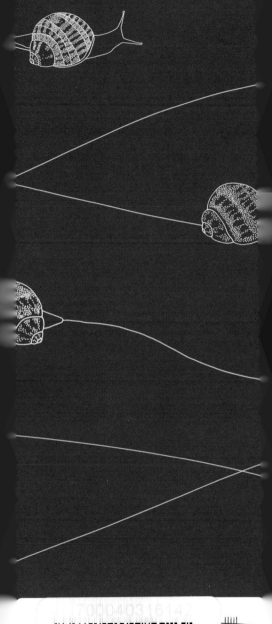

A Slow Passion

A Slow Passion

Snails, My Garden and Me

RUTH BROOKS

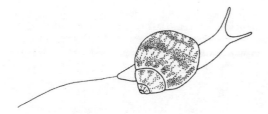

B L O O M S B U R Y

LONDON • NEW DELHI • NEW YORK • SYDNEY

For my children,
Matthew, Sarah, Yvette and Nathan

First published in Great Britain 2013

Text copyright © 2013 by Ruth Brooks
Illustrations © 2013 by Claire Hartigan

Bloomsbury Publishing Plc, 50 Bedford Square, London WC1B 3DP

Bloomsbury Publishing, London, New Delhi, New York and Sydney

A CIP catalogue record for this book is available from the British Library

ISBN 978 1 4088 2658 4

Typeset by Hewer Text UK Ltd, Edinburgh
Printed and Bound in Great Britain by CPI (UK) Ltd, Croydon CR0 4YY

Illustrations by Claire Hartigan,
www.clairehartigan.com

10 9 8 7 6 5 4 3 2 1

www.bloomsbury.com/ruthbrooks

Considering the Snail

The snail pushes through a green
night, for the grass is heavy
with water and meets over
the bright path he makes, where rain
has darkened the earth's dark. He
moves in a wood of desire,

pale antlers barely stirring
as he hunts. I cannot tell
what power is at work, drenched there
with purpose, knowing nothing.
What is a snail's fury? All
I think is that if later

I parted the blades above
the tunnel and saw the thin
trail of broken white across
litter, I would never have
imagined the slow passion
to that deliberate progress.

Thom Gunn

Contents

Contents

Introduction

How ingenious an animal is a snail. When it encounters
a bad neighbour, it takes up its house and moves away.

(Philemon, c.300BC)

My four-year-old grandson, Robert, reached down into the muddy depths of my garden pond. He sat back on his heels, clutching something in a tight fist. Slowly, he opened his hand. Glistening wetly black on his palm was the cone-shaped shell of a water snail. Robert's eyes sparkled with curiosity. He poked and prodded the snail, tracing the curves of its shell with his finger. The creature nestled in his palm like a precious gem displayed on a tiny pink cushion. Proudly, he held out his treasure for us all to admire.

Sunlight flooded my garden in Totnes, Devon. It was June 2010. My daughter, Sarah, son-in-law, Chris, grandson, Robert and twenty-month-old granddaughter, Elizabeth, gathered round the pond. Placed at strategic intervals, each of us jealously guarding our own strait of water, our mission that afternoon was to clear all the duckweed from the surface.

Somewhere beneath its carpet were tadpoles, their limbs not yet fully formed, almost ready to climb the sloping concrete sides and explore the garden. A flotilla of water-lilies breathed in new oxygen as we eased the weed from beneath their stems and flower heads.

Toddlers and ponds do not combine well. Before the children came to stay, I had laid planks across the water, covered with strong netting, leaving a few narrow gaps at the edge for dipping into. Swirling our hands round at the edges, we scooped up handfuls of duckweed, finding dozens of tadpoles enmeshed in them. Releasing them was a delicate balancing act – a job for the grown-ups. We had to peel most of the weed away from each tiny blob of black jelly, then, keeping hold of the bit of greenery with the tadpole still on top, nudge the animal back into the water. This simple activity, repeated again and again, was so meditatively relaxing that I wished the afternoon could last for ever. In my store of family recollections, I hold this particular memory – *my* treasure – aloft. Like so many of my happiest memories, it is connected with a garden.

In my Devon garden, with its open, south-facing views across a valley, my family and other city visitors visibly relax, for a while shedding their daily cares. Blinking in the sunshine, they seem both bemused and dazzled by their surroundings. Steeply rising hills tilt their green-gold faces towards the morning sun. Sheep graze on these sloping fields criss-crossed with ancient hedgerows, their fleeces stained pink by the red Devon earth. The river Dart is hidden from my sight beneath the folds of the hills, yet I always feel its presence. In autumn, as I sit up in bed with my early-morning cup of tea, I see Canada geese fly past in their perfect V, honking and soaring above the river.

Here, the seasons unfold in miniature, displaying their ever-changing colours and patterns of light and shadow. Come spring, friends call round to swap seeds; in the summer, they take away some of my abundant crop of blackcurrants, half of which will be returned to me in jars of delicious jam. Neighbouring children, clutching nets and buckets, dip into my pond for spare tadpoles to be transferred to new ponds or to tanks on kitchen window ledges.

Animals visit my garden, too. Butterflies, bees, wasps and dragonflies come to call, then fly away with a whirr of wings. Seagulls swoop overhead, their hungry screech such a part of my waking-up routine that I miss it dreadfully when I'm away. Some visitors are not so welcome. Squirrels with determined claws and teeth tear holes in my bird feeders and eat the sunflower seeds. Sometimes I see a rat streaking across my patio before squeezing under the neighbour's fence. Its live appearance is much more unsettling than the stone-dead offerings my cats leave on the doorstep.

Certain earthbound visitors love my garden so much that they have taken up residence, as if in the belief that they are lords of all they survey. Blending into the landscape, they creep about, intent on their daily business. These intriguing animals populate every flower bed and vegetable patch. Sometimes, in the dead of night, they even gain entry into my house, leaving behind their signature silvery trails.

The snails and I go back a long way. We have had a chequered relationship. When I was four years old, my best friend and I used to have snail races. We marvelled at the ingenious way in which they moved along on their own rivers of slime; at their pinhead eyes, which, when we touched them, disappeared down the hollow stalks of their tentacles. We loved the little animals and would play with them for hours. Throughout my childhood, this interest never waned. Only later, when I owned a garden for the first time, did my ardour fade beneath layers of fury and desperation. Often, I was certain that my snails would drive me insane.

Snails are destructive blighters. They have a penchant for any plant that is tender, young and juicy. They make a beeline for the graceful delphinium – centrepiece of my summer bedding – and for the lettuce seedlings that I have nurtured for weeks with the sweat of my brow. They also have rapacious jaws. Sometimes, in the stillness of night, I have heard these at work. Snails have thousands of minute teeth, arranged in rows like the spikes on a rasp. These rows, forming a square, often appear as rectangular indentations on my cabbage leaves. Every year, I bemoan the destruction that takes place in my vegetable patch. And every year, I hear similar tales of woe and frustration from fellow gardeners.

Gardening is the national pastime. Snails are the national pest. How to reconcile these two opposing forces? In the past, I was a snail slaughterer, with no mercy or conscience. For a brief time, I used deadly metaldehyde pellets, but how I hated removing the twisted, greenish corpses that lay strewn across the killing fields of my vegetable patch. Gradually, I converted to organic methods of control, but these were expensive and time-consuming – and often I ended up still killing the beasts. Whatever I did, it never felt quite right.

Slowly, I realised that I couldn't put my heart into all this destruction. I *liked* my snails. More than that, I was still fascinated by them. They had been on this planet for about six hundred million years, far longer than us humans. As far as I knew, they didn't kill one another, or eat each other. They were, in their own way, elegant, even beautiful, with their intricate shells and delicate features. The excitement I had felt as a child returned with new vigour.

As I pottered about my garden in that summer of 2010, I began to observe my snails more closely. I had often wondered what that second set of tentacles – the tiny ones, below the eye stalks – was for. I learnt that they were for sniffing out their food. I could see them waving about as the snails slimed perilously close to my lettuces. If snails had a sense of smell, then they were not so different from creatures belonging to higher mammalian orders. Umpteen preservation societies exist to protect our favourite species: whales and dolphins, elephants and retired donkeys. Yet snails, in most people's eyes, are lowly creatures.

Common sense told me that I was being downright foolish to get steamed up about the fate of an animal that seemed little more than a garden pest. It didn't worry me that other people might consider me eccentric, but I needed to justify to myself my fondness for my snails. Was I being unwise, or even deluded, in championing the cause of the tiny creature that was chomping its way merrily through my runner-bean seedlings? To find out, I first needed to get all my facts straight.

I dug out old nature guides on garden wildlife. I prowled round my garden, identifying different types of snails, amazed at how many different species could inhabit one small plot. Each was a small work of art. The white-lipped banded snail had a shiny, creamy shell with five dark, evenly spaced bands. I found one curled up in a clump of grass. Plainly it wasn't after my vegetables, but was minding its own business in its usual resting place. At the bottom of my hedge nestled a snail whose shell reminded me of a prim Victorian schoolmarm's hairdo. It had a neat topknot at the apex, creamy amber, spiralling elegantly into a perfect point. This was the Kentish snail, and it wasn't after my seedlings either: it preferred decaying vegetation. The tiniest of all, the garlic glass-snail, had a brown shell just seven millimetres across. I found it in the leaf mould I had swept up in the autumn, under logs and in my compost heap. It fed on fungi, worms, insects and grubs – not on fresh vegetables at all.

With shock and a sense of shame, I realised that I had been zapping all the snails in my garden indiscriminately, viewing them all as pests waging war on me. Most were relatively harmless, peacefully inhabiting hedgerows and wild areas. Yet, with my deadly pellets, I had probably enticed them out of their hidey-holes, upsetting the balance of nature in the ecosystem that was my garden.

For years, I had been familiar with the terms 'environment' and 'ecology' without knowing the distinction between them or understanding how they applied to my own personal world. Disappearing rainforests, melting ice caps and declining bee populations were frightening to contemplate, yet I had felt strangely detached from them. Now, it was becoming clear to me that whatever was happening on my own patch of ground, it reflected, in miniature, the bigger picture 'out there'. I had a sense of things being out of balance, and that I was playing a part in this disharmony.

The snails in my garden were symbols of a great divide, a battle for survival between pest and plant. So wide was the gulf between the two that almost all the gardening magazines and books I read devoted articles and chapters to pest control. Yet snails and lettuces were both inhabitants of my garden, each doing their best to survive. All those years of battling snails had left me weary and jaded. Killing, controlling, obsessing – all this had left a dark stain on my psyche. It felt wrong. *I* felt wrong. There must be a better solution to the Great Snail Problem, and I felt a responsibility to find it. More than anything else, I wanted to feel at ease with myself.

Once our basic needs – food, shelter and warmth – are met, we still hunger for something more. To experience beauty, in whatever form, lifts our spirits and nourishes us. Our individual ideals may be subjective, but some experiences seem universal. All of us, at some time, have stopped still and caught our breath while viewing stars on a clear, still night, or marvelled at the spiralled petal formation of a flower. On an icy morning, I am amazed by the myriad frost patterns on the windscreens of the cars parked in my road. I know that there is a scientific reason for their delicate and intricate designs, yet they still seem miraculous – like snowflakes. When I was a child, in the severe winter of 1947, my school friends and I would try to catch these gifts from the sky, as they fell silently onto the school playground or rested for a fleeting moment on sleeves and hats. When we were told by the teacher that every snowflake was different, I refused to believe her. Even now, I cannot believe that something so exquisite can manifest itself again and again in billions of different guises.

My snails taught me how to be still and once again to catch my breath in wonder. They opened me up to the natural world. For years, I had been viewing all the creatures in my garden – the worms, the grubs and the snails – from the height of a human being. Work, family and pressures of all kinds meant that my gardening often happened in frenzied bouts. I'd weed and plant in a whirlwind of activity, always with an eye on my watch, always planning ahead: the next meal; tomorrow's work schedule. My mind was rarely on what I was doing, let alone the rich variety of wildlife that inhabited the earth about my plants. Beneath my fingers was a thoroughfare of microorganisms, all going about their important tasks, all keeping my soil healthy and forming part of the food chain. While I forked over the earth in autumn, a robin watched eagerly from a nearby fence post, waiting for me to upturn a tasty, wriggling worm.

My snails, too, were hiding in the garden, looking for their meal. I needed a completely new strategy to protect my runner-bean seedlings. I wanted to still the chattering in my mind that told me these common garden snails were public enemy number one. The only way to do this was to get down to their height, to lie down on my front and enter their world. This was a ground-level kingdom, where pebbles were massive boulders and flowerpots sheer cliff faces. Sliming across the smooth slabs of my patio was the equivalent of running a marathon; the shadow of my hand was a dark storm cloud threatening danger. I watched the snails curl up in fright, only to emerge from their shells a little while later, one tentacle at a time, the tiny eyes waving round on their stalks, reassuring them that their terrain was safe again. I noticed the translucent shells of the juveniles and their perfectly formed little bodies. They looked so fragile. I wondered how their houses stayed intact when they retreated into the abrasive cracks and crevices that provided their night-time resting places.

I became, once more, like a child. I observed the graceful way the snails glided along. I saw the two lower stalks on their heads waving about as they scented food, and forgot for a moment that they were streaking towards my prize hostas. In the stillness of that moment, my garden, with all its creatures, became a place of tiny miracles. I discovered that everything was connected. Once again, I felt that spark, that fascination with the garden and its inhabitants that began when I was four years old, the same excitement that I would see reflected in the eyes of my grandson as he dipped into my pond. There, in my own small plot of land, a whole new world awaited me; except that, in truth, this was my old world, one that for years I had almost forgotten. That summer, as I became involved in some absorbing and challenging research, I reconnected with my childhood self.

Snail Races

s four-year-old children, my friend Mary and I were too young to play outside on the small round green in the centre of our close – Mary's mother was very firm about that. Yet her dire warning was unnecessary. In 1945, there were only three cars in the close, including my father's. His battered old Austin 7 arriving home at five miles an hour, with revs noisy enough to scatter a whole playground of children, was hardly a threat to our safety. But we did as we were told, and instead would peer through the wooden slats of the front gate, watching the big children riding their bikes round and round on the road or careering along on their roller skates.

Mary and I lived in Watford, Hertfordshire. In those days, it was a genteel, sleepy town. On shopping trips, our car would bump along the old, cobbled streets at the lower end of the High Street. Here were the unglamorous, utilitarian stores: the bike shop that sold second-hand bicycles and tyre-mending kits; the electrician's, where you could buy a short length of fuse wire or a twin-tub washing machine. On Saturday afternoons, while my father browsed among the light fittings, my mother would treat me to Victoria sponge cake and orange juice in the Queen's Pantry, an olde worlde tea shop with red-and-white-checked seersucker tablecloths and huge oak beams. Later, we would shop in Clements, the department store, where canisters laden with small change jangled and whizzed along overhead cables, like something out of *Charlie and the Chocolate Factory* (youngsters under sixty will not remember this ingenious way of transporting coins, receipts and dockets from one cash desk to another – they're convinced you must be spinning a yarn).

Our close, too, was peaceful and quiet, a cluster of ten semi-detached houses. They were arranged in a semicircle, and so were all the back gardens. None of them was your regular suburban rectangle. My next-door neighbour's was twice as wide as deep. Next door to Mary's, Mrs Jackson's plot, where we used to hunt for four-leaved clovers, was like a small field; viewed from her back door, it fell away into wild, grassy meadowland. The two end gardens, Mary's included, were triangular and small, but to us her garden was a world in itself, our adventure playground.

Mary's mother left us alone to play our highly imaginative games, with deckchair dens and mud-pie dinners for our dolls. We lived in the moment, without a thought to consequences, and there was plenty to tempt us into mischief. We turned on the outside tap and, shrieking, showered each other with freezing water from the hosepipe.

We ended up soaked through, from the smocked bodices of our gingham frocks down to our white socks and Clarks sandals. Warm, sudsy foam would suddenly gush into a drain from the washing machine and, as we paddled in it, we pretended we were at the seaside. A clammy toad lived under a stone. When we woke it up, instead of leaping away, it froze in terror, while we stared, fascinated by the rapid heartbeat in its flanks. We marvelled at its tiny hands, with perfect fingers just like ours. If we scraped between the paving stones with a stick, black streams of ants would erupt from the cracks. Sometimes, horrid little girls that we were, we'd stamp on them. Creatures intrigued us, but we had not yet learnt to respect them.

We spent every spare minute in that garden, exploring its varied terrain and textures. We wheeled our dolls' prams round and round the patio outside the French windows. Our jungle was the prickly thicket of brambles that straggled against the end fence. To us, this was a menacing bush. We invested that bramble with a magical quality. It was a bad fairy whose nasty prickles would cast an evil spell on us if we touched it, just like the needle in *Sleeping Beauty*. The graceful buddleja, by contrast, was a good fairy. Its fragrant flower heads made pillows for our dolls, or posh wedding hats for our hair.

Trees and plants lit up our imagination, yet it was the world of tiny creatures that appealed the most – particularly that of the snails. All the snails in the neighbourhood seemed to congregate in Mary's garden. They hid in cracks and crevices and under flowerpots, where they slowly awoke from their winter hibernation. For reasons we never understood, in my garden there were none to be found. One particular day, having just finished the mud pies and wiped our soggy hands down our dresses, we were rushing up and down the grassy mound over the old air-raid shelter, shouting 'I'm the king of the castle' and seeing who could jump furthest down the slope from the very top. As always, Mary won. She was lighter and more graceful than me, like a baby gazelle. I was more like a baby elephant.

I heard and felt a sickening crunch as I landed on something fragile – a snail shell. Immediately, we stopped jumping and crouched down to inspect the damage.

'You've squashed it,' Mary accused. 'It's deaded!'

'No I haven't!' I turned the snail upside down. 'Look – there's nothing inside it.'

I held out the empty shell, now concertinaed into several fragments. 'Let's find some alive ones and have races!'

We knew exactly where to find our athletes. Previous snail hunts had taught us that at night, snails slept under rocks and plant pots; during the day, they travelled to the nearest tasty plant. At the base of the air-raid shelter were several clumps of primulas with half-eaten petals, and hidden among them was a colony of snails. Within minutes, we'd collected handfuls of them. Our favourites were the juveniles, with their translucent shells. We always counted their whorls first. One whorl, a complete circle within the spiral of each shell, meant that it was one year old, two whorls meant that it was two, and so on – or so we believed.

Lining up our racers a few yards from the primulas, we gave the juniors a head start. We always left the biggest snails alone. These were the parents, the grown-ups. And grown-ups didn't play. Their job was to stay at home and get the tea ready for when the races were over. Besides, the bigger snails were slower and lazier. Sometimes, they couldn't be bothered even to come out of their shells. They looked asleep – or dead. Once, we turned a couple of these upside down and found that the entrance to their shells was sealed up with something that felt and looked like Sellotape. These were the hibernating snails, still sealed up in their protective skins, not yet ready to brave the chilly April sunshine. Mary used to say that they were like her dad, asleep with the newspaper over his head.

The first one to find its way home through the long grass was the winner. But they were an unruly lot. They moved surprisingly fast for their size, but they kept going off at a tangent.

'Go on, go *on*!' Mary urged. 'Back to the flowers. Your mummies and daddies will worry about you.'

A minute, slimy black sausage extruded from beneath several of the creatures.

'Is that poo?' I asked eagerly, poking the sticky substance with my finger. 'Ugh – it's disgusting!'

'How do they know how to get home?' Mary worried. 'They look lost.'

'They know, because they have a brain,' I said.

I wasn't sure precisely what a brain was. But I did know that it was a very useful thing to have. Every morning, my mother told me I should use it, when I put my shoe on the wrong foot.

'I can't see a brain,' Mary said, frowning.

'That's because it's under its shell.'

'I don't believe you!' Mary peered, her nose level with the side of the shell. 'There isn't room under there.'

'It's in their tummy, then.'

We settled on this theory, content to watch in silence as the baby snails navigated their way across the lawn. At last, some of them made it back to the primula patch, no doubt, we imagined, to a joyous reunion with their anxious parents. Little did I realise, at the tender age of four, that I'd just conducted my first snail homing experiment.

TWO

My Childhood Garden

The games we played as children, the plants and wildlife we discovered, confirmed my view that any garden, whoever it belonged to, was the most exciting place in which to be. Out in the fresh air, my spirits rose, I felt free, unfettered. Houses were boring – even other people's. Within their four walls, I felt trapped, stultified, and couldn't wait to explore outside. I loved seeing how my friends' parents wove their individual tastes and personalities into the different designs of their gardens, creating so many variations on what was usually one medium-sized rectangle. Goldfish swam in lily-carpeted ponds, cabbages and sprouts flourished in vegetable patches, dainty pink and mauve alpines snuggled between boulders in rockeries.

All these were new to me, as my garden had none of these features. In one friend's garden there grew a mature European larch, as tall as a church spire. I thought it was the most beautiful tree I had ever seen, with its graceful, wide-sweeping branches and bright green leaves. I admired its spaciousness and elegance. A larch, I decided, would be an amazing addition to our garden, the envy of all our neighbours. I pleaded with my mother to find out where we could buy a young sapling. 'Don't they grow rather high?' she asked, doubtfully. 'Where on earth would we put it?'

The summer of 1952 lingers in my mind, freshly evocative with its scents of new-mown grass and old roses and my own sun-tanned skin. Memory encapsulates into one powerful soundscape the lazy drones of lawnmowers and bees, and the sonorous cooing of a wood pigeon. The colours of the perennials glow even more vividly: the deep pinks of gladioli and the varied purples of lavender and asters. Imagining is much better than going back to my childhood home, although I've had opportunities to do so – old friends still live nearby. The house was sold long ago, and each new owner has no doubt put an individual stamp on it. I have no wish to see how it has been altered. I want to remember everything just as it was.

At the age of eleven, I sometimes still played in Mary's garden on the opposite side of our close, but I had discovered new delights in my own garden, and often she would come over at weekends or after school. My garden was a pentagon. The two boundary fences on each side fanned out at an angle. The back fence had a kink in the middle, pointing outwards, making even more space. It opened up a shallow, boggy triangle, in which stood a giant gunnera with huge leaves like monster hands. The fence backed onto four other gardens, a fact which for some reason never failed to impress visiting relatives. Near the gunnera grew an old cooking-apple tree with gnarled, spreading branches. It was perfect for climbing and for retreating into when I'd had a row with someone or other. A dilapidated garden shed beside the apple tree housed an ancient lawnmower and a lot of junk. This was the wild part of the garden, which I loved best of all.

The back door opened onto a path, a safe place to practise my roller skating where the neighbours couldn't see me (balance was never my strong point). It was fringed with a bed of lavender that gave off a divine scent. In summer, I picked bunches of it, and secretly – or so I believed – hung them upside down in my wardrobe, with the intention, at some later date, of making them into embroidered, linen-wrapped posies: birthday and Christmas gifts for my friends and my mother. Usually I forgot, but my wardrobe smelt delightful. Beyond the path was a large lawn, and this led down to the wild part of the garden, its entrance guarded by two tall cypress trees standing either side.

My garden, although not huge, was larger than the average suburban garden. The wide central flower bed would have done justice to any stately home. Here flourished all the perennials, together with a strange interloper: a single gooseberry bush, fruiting faithfully year after year amid the clumps of goldenrod, asters, Michaelmas-daisies and majestic gladioli. Sweet-scented lilies-of-the-valley lined the edge of the bed, spilling onto the lawn, which ran along its length. The flower bed was so large that weeding was a mammoth task. Ideally, it had to be completed in one fell swoop. If some of it was left even for a week, new weeds popped up. As this job was always done in fits and starts, we never had the satisfaction of admiring a mass of colourful blooms set against freshly raked bare earth.

A rough path, paved with concrete slabs interspersed with a mass of dandelions and cracks, led to the entrance of the old air-raid shelter. Previous owners had had it built before the war, and it was a feature in many gardens during the war years – although Mary's was the only other family in our close to possess one. Steps disappeared down into a dark concrete cell, eight feet by six feet. The single pre-1940 light bulb still worked perfectly. It revealed rusty iron bunk beds draped with cobwebs and spiders. I have dim memories of being snatched out of my warm bed as a baby in the dead of night, and hustled down into this shelter, wrapped in my eiderdown, while distant bombs exploded.

Mary and I sometimes dared each other to go down there. One day, after Mary had gone home, I steeled myself to venture down alone. Deliberately, I didn't switch on the light, breathing in the dank, earthy air while I waited for my eyes to adjust to the dim light filtering through two tiny grilles. After a few moments, I realised that I had company. Clinging to the large damp patches that stained the walls, a colony of snails had made its way down into the darkness, to escape the summer heat. They huddled close together, shells touching, as if seeking comfort from one another. They were stuck there, some on the wall, some upside down on the ceiling, perfectly still. I wondered how they got out of here to find their food, and how long it took them. Did they talk to each other, in their own snailish way? They must have had a miserable existence down here in the damp and the gloom.

I stroked their shells, each as different in its speckled brown markings as the hairstyles and faces of my friends at school. It was comforting to have other creatures keeping me company, even if they weren't at all sociable. This was a place for making up ghost stories, but there was too much fear there already. In this dark, silent cave, haunted by the terrors of war, I could still hear the soft boom of the bombs. Long after the war, my mother told me that a house in the next street had been destroyed completely. I had no recollection of the event, but a ghostly, felt memory lingered: the splintering crash of bomb-blasted windows, which sent shivers along my spine. From the safety of 1952, in the light of day, the war seemed like a history lesson. It didn't touch my life. Only down there, in the shelter, did it become real again.

I couldn't wait to scramble out into the safe, sunlit world of my garden. But it had been worth it. The next day, I'd have the satisfaction of boasting to my friend that I'd been down there all on my own.

Mary and I much preferred to play on top of the shelter, running up and down the grassy mound that formed its roof. An isolated peach tree grew on the shelter's summit. My mother simply left it alone. There were no chemical sprays in those days, but it never got blight. When it bothered to fruit, every few years, it rewarded us with the most delicious peaches. Sometimes we'd climb it, but it was small and compact, tame compared to the old apple tree, our greatest challenge. On the lower slopes of the mound grew clusters of white and yellow alyssum, which flowered year after year, together with primulas and cowslips.

My garden's main feature was the big lawn with long, lush grass, setting off to perfection the varied shapes and colours of the summer bedding all around it. The grass was mown only when my father, with a sigh, dragged the old mower out of the shed and trundled slowly up and down. As I listened to the pleasant rasping drone of the rotating blades, I loved to watch the broad grassy stripes appear gradually across the lawn in alternating shades of green.

Between this lawn and the wild area at the bottom of the garden was another huge bed, where roses bloomed. They were my mother's pride and joy. I could catch the intoxicating scent from yards away. These were old-variety roses, deep crimson with huge, blowsy flower heads and velvety petals. My favourites were smaller and peach-coloured, at their most exquisite just before the petals fully unfolded. They bloomed year after year: my mother knew exactly what they needed. She did very little, except to cut them down sharply every February so that just a few inches of thorny stub stuck up through the soil.

My mother had the greenest fingers of anyone I have ever known. She was an artist, a painter and sculptor. She knew a hundred shades of each colour of the rainbow, and she had a tube of oil paint for each one. Words such as 'viridian', 'cadmium yellow', 'burnt umber' and 'aquamarine' were as ordinary during my childhood as 'pen' and 'pencil'. My mother loved flowers with a fierce passion, made all the more poignant because plants didn't like her in return.

At first, she had believed that household cleaning fluids were the cause of her periodic episodes of severe skin allergy, when her hands erupted in great weals and scabs that would sometimes spread over her whole body. She always wore rubber gloves when she washed up, vigorously attacking the greasy breakfast plates with a dishcloth, her shiny, unmade-up morning face a comical mix of distaste, impatience and resignation. Housework was not my mother's thing. She was a reluctant Fifties housewife, buying *Good Housekeeping* purely for the fashion pages and recipes – hearty exhortations to feed her children with cod-liver oil and malt to supplement the lean diet of the post-war years. Mending torn sheets and frayed shirt cuffs left her cold. Yet, like many mothers of her time, she had become a victim of journalistic propaganda to get women back into the home after their brief flurry of independence as land girls and munitions workers. When my mother washed up, her whole body seemed to sag and shrink into itself. Her cheeks lost their delicate pink bloom and her features became pale and pinched. Even her hair, normally jet black and shiny, hung in straggly, lacklustre strands. Her eyes, emerald green and sparkling when she worked on her paintings, turned as grey as the cooking pots in the sink. None of my friends had a mother whose eyes changed colour according to her mood.

In spite of all the precautions she took inside the house to protect her skin, she gaily sallied out into the garden without ever wearing her gardening gloves, because she loved the soft touch of petals on her skin, particularly the velvet of her roses. She never guessed, as she weeded and pruned and garnered, that some deadly poison lurked among the summer bedding. For my mother, this could have been fatal.

I remember the last time she came into contact with the allergen, when I was nine years old. Her skin erupted into the worst, most life-threatening rash she had ever suffered. When I visited her in hospital she was bandaged from head to foot, even her head and face, leaving two small holes for her eyes. My mummy had turned into an Egyptian mummy. It hurt her to speak, because the rash had gone inside, too, into every part of her body, and as she croaked a greeting to me, I gripped the sides of the iron bedstead so hard that there were red streaks across my palms for hours afterwards. She was in an isolation ward, a little room that stank of disinfectant and starched sheets. It was scarily tidy and clinically clean, so unlike the familiar untidiness of home. Solicitous nurses spoke in hushed, gentle voices, and all their movements were slow and careful as they lifted the bandages on her arms to dab calamine lotion onto her raw, red flesh.

She spent weeks in hospital. Then, when she came home, she was in bed for what seemed like months, covered in ugly scabs that itched all the time. The house reeked of calamine, which she splashed onto her skin every hour of the day and night.

I cannot remember whether she had any allergy tests during her stay in hospital. Certainly such tests were not as efficient and sophisticated as they are today. But by now my mother had put two and two together. The culprits were hiding somewhere amid the plants. As much as she loved those plants, she had to keep away.

After this, I rarely saw her in the garden. She went outside to hang up the washing or pick a few roses, or to decorate the edges of the beds and paths with stones and shells in the quirky way she enjoyed. These were artefacts that she had secreted in the boot of the car as mementoes from our seaside holidays, where she would spend hours sketching and painting. To me, they seemed strange bedfellows for the rough gravel or earth that surrounded them. Yet arranging her stones and shells was the only way she could be, safely, in her beloved garden. She stooped down, half-kneeling on a bristly doormat, dressed in the shabby, mismatched clothes she wore round the house – clothes she would not have been seen dead in if visitors had called. Bundled round her waist was a bright floral apron with a large pocket for the shells and scissors and clothes pegs. It was a terrible thing for her, to give up something she loved so much. The stones might have satisfied her need for beauty. But they were mere objects, inert and lifeless. Her own vitality longed to connect with the living world.

Neither could my father help. He wasn't the least interested in plants, and rarely ventured outside. He had another reason for not gardening. He had been badly injured in the war, and heavy physical work was beyond him. He looked healthy enough, with a ruddy complexion and no visible disabilities, but all his injuries were internal. These were savage, secret wounds, never to be spoken of. 'Don't mention the war.' It was a silent, complicit agreement between my mother and myself, long before anyone else coined the phrase. It was as much as he could do to mow the lawn, which he did slowly and stiffly, mopping his brow in the afternoon heat, pausing now and again to adjust the large handkerchief on top of his head. This was carefully knotted at the corners, in my father's meticulous way, to protect his head from the sun. Besides, he too had an allergy, although it wasn't nearly as bad as my mother's. At the start of the summer, as soon as a pollen grain wafted through the kitchen window, he would sneeze his head off, usually for ten minutes at a time. The man who lived in the house at the bottom of the garden had the same problem, and often they would sneeze together, in a series of explosions that ricocheted round the back gardens like farmers taking pot shots at rabbits.

The garden was full of weeds, since my mother had given up working in it. Yet I loved it. I was out there whenever I could escape the stuffiness of our kitchen, where our grey marble-effect stove was constantly stoked up to provide hot water for washing. I would hunt round to see what was growing in each season. In spring, I absorbed the abundant progression of snowdrops, crocuses, daffodils. Tulips would follow, then pinks, yellow alyssum and purple aubretia. My favourite was the aquilegia, with its delicate stems and pastel shades of mauve and pink. I hated it when they faded away. It felt like a tiny death inside me, too. For a while, the earth looked bare and forlorn, and I longed for the dazzling display of summer perennials, old faithfuls that came up every year, such as lupins, goldenrod, calendula and elegant purple irises.

Somehow it never occurred to me to do the weeding for my mother, or to ask for my own small patch of earth. I was too active. My whole body ached to move, but not to be straitjacketed by tiny weeding and planting movements. I craved the freedom of wild sweeps and whirls and jumps. I wanted to test the strength of my body, to push it to its limits. So Mary and I now developed a new passion – gymnastics – and my garden, with all its space and possibilities, was our gymnasium.

My mother's roses and the summer perennials, rising triumphant among the weeds, formed the backdrop to our handstands and cartwheels, and the long grass – our floor mat – was a soft landing. The old apple tree was perfect for swinging by our arms: two branches formed our parallel bars, through which we flipped feet first, clinging on to the branch above, then let go, curving Tarzan-like in a graceful back arch down onto the soft earth below. We would give each other marks out of ten for a correct, no-wobbles landing.

When this seemed too tame, we jumped across the stairwell of the air-raid shelter, daring each other to leap across the widest gap. After a few bruises and hard landings, we hauled the flowerpots out of the shed. These were proper earthenware pots – plastic ones never darkened our shed door in those days. We'd line up twenty pots of different sizes and heights, then, gradually increasing the distance between them, jump from one to the next. The winner was the one who completed the course without falling off.

The coal bunker against the end wall of the garage provided an extreme form of long jump as we leapt from the top. We aimed at a skipping-rope line a few feet away, moving it further each time. Then Mary would run home to get her own skipping rope, and we'd do bumps. This was twice as hard as ordinary skipping, as the rope had to pass twice under our feet as we jumped high in the air, turning the rope with a quick double flick of the wrists. We counted each other's bumps – if we missed one, or got caught up in the rope, we had to start all over again. It took hours of practice to reach more than fifty non-stop bumps.

After this, it was positively relaxing to do handstands against my neighbour's fence. I could feel the warmth of the sun on my bare legs as they flashed through the air, and it felt good. Everything felt good in the garden.

My five-year-old sister, Susan, created a new dimension to our play. She was too young for our organised games and more strenuous gymnastics, and usually she played with her own friends. But sometimes she was at a loose end, and, in that irritatingly condescending way of most elder sisters, I sometimes included her in our games. We taught her handstands and cartwheels and somersaults. We'd play wheelbarrows, lifting her thighs while she scrambled forward on her hands. Hide-and-seek was a favourite. We pretended not to see her peering anxiously from behind the cypress trees and, on purpose, took ages to find her. We swung her so high on the newly installed swing that she screamed with fear and delight.

Mary envied me, having a cute little sister with black hair, dark solemn eyes and skin as silky as rose petals. I loved Susan dearly, but I also envied Mary, because she had a brother. Even better, he was five years older, which was practically grown up. He was away most of the time at a boarding school with a reputation for being very strict. In my eyes, this gave him a mysterious and faintly tragic air. I had a terrible crush on him – from a safe distance – and used to go bright red if he spoke to me.

I was not a gardener in any practical sense. What mattered most to my eleven-year-old self was the sheer joy of being outside in the fresh air, and seeing the different plants that seemed magically to pop through the soil when I wasn't looking. After Mary or other school friends had gone home, I would linger in the cool of the evening, always reluctant to go inside, searching round to see what was new. I loved anything unexpected or unusual. In one particular flower bed grew different shrubs punctuated by a hotchpotch of wild escapes, plants that had somehow seeded themselves from elsewhere. My favourites were the wood spurge and the yellow oxalis. As soon as I saw the yellowish, umbel-like clusters of the spurge, I knew that summer was just a cuckoo-call away (people wrote to *The Times* when they heard the cuckoo's first call in May, so I imagined it must be very important).

May was my favourite month, the cherry and apple trees wearing their ballerina dresses of blossom. I loved looking up into the beech trees, where sunlight sparkled amid the delicate pale green leaves as if through a lacy shawl. The cuckoo also heralded June, with its long summer evenings, when we could play outside late. Then, at last, would come the summer holidays, with no school for six weeks. In those days, summer seemed to stretch for ever.

I delighted in plants that had the added value of fun. Although I was eleven, my need for silly, inconsequential play was as strong as ever. Near the French windows flourished a mature snowberry bush. If I picked handfuls of these white berries, threw them to the ground, then stamped on them, they made a satisfying popping sound, even better than bubble-wrap. I knew it was called a snowberry, just as I knew the names of all the perennials. Effortlessly, I'd absorbed this knowledge from my mother, and the words 'goldenrod', 'snap-dragon', 'lavender' sang in my head like the lyrics of a well-loved song. But the actual naming of plants was not important to me – the garden was a place for dreams and stories and play. But this would soon change. The garden was to become my responsibility.

THREE

Spark of Inspiration

y youngest sister was born on Christmas Eve, in 1953, when I was thirteen. Like my sister Susan, six years earlier, Lucy brought joy to the whole family. By the summer, she was sturdy enough to be plonked on a mat in the middle of the lawn, propped up with cushions, where she'd sit with her chubby legs tucked beneath her, blinking with amazement at the wide, bright world that surrounded her.

I soon adopted the duties of a sensible older sister, babysitting while my parents went out and keeping an eagle eye open for any tiny, dangerous object that might be lurking within her reach. To compensate, Lucy gave me a perfect excuse for behaving much younger than befitted a thirteen-year-old. Susan and I spent hours crawling round her on the grass, playing peep-bo, making silly faces and introducing Lucy to the delights of the garden. We'd bring, for her solemn inspection, the large, smooth stones that my mother always brought back from seaside holidays, fir cones from the cypresses and tree bark – anything she couldn't swallow whole that was not poisonous. We'd waft lavender and rose petals under her nose to watch it twitch, and tickle her chin with buttercups to see if she loved butter. Our daisy chains garlanded her little chest, and she'd try to stuff these, together with all the other flowers we showed her, into her mouth.

My mother was now fully stretched with feeds and nappy changes, shopping and cooking and washing. Her allergy already restricted the amount of gardening she did; now she had barely the time or the energy to do even the minimum. In the back, the perennials still popped up, the apple tree was laden with delicious cookers, the roses bloomed, the gooseberry bush offered up its tartly sweet fruits. Yet the whole garden was a jungle of weeds.

It wasn't until the following summer that I decided I could bear it no longer: the garden looked so sad and neglected. It cried out for tender loving care. One day, I found a rusty hand fork and trowel in the shed, and strode towards the central flower bed. I began by clearing a space round the gooseberry bush, where Susan was still half-convinced we had found Lucy. Vigorously, I attacked the dandelions, fat-hen and other deep-rooted weeds, soon finding that hand tools were useless. I ran back to the shed and found an even rustier fork and spade. I had to jump onto the edges of these to force them down deep enough to clear the bottom of the roots. I was amazed how deep they grew. Soon, I had a small pile. I was sweating with the effort, yet it was satisfying – like an extreme form of the gymnastics I loved so much. After this, pulling up the gently yielding groundsel was a sensuous delight. By teatime, I'd cleared at least a tenth of the whole bed.

I was hooked. The more I did, the more I could see was yet to be done. During tea that evening, my mind was racing with plans for the garden. I was a gardener in the making. The next day, with a new, critical eye, I surveyed the central bed again. The goldenrod and Michaelmas-daisies were taking over. They had been there ever since I could remember, and they were old hat. This led to my first attempts at Thinning Out. My plan was to divide them and put bits of them down in the wild, boggy, shaded part of the garden, where the apple tree and gunnera grew. There was little colour down there and the whole area needed brightening up. I was totally ignorant about plant preferences for shade or sunshine. I tried to divide the daisies by pulling hard at the outer stems, never having seen the spade method of division, whereby two spades, back-to-back, are dug into the centre of the clump and then forced apart. All that happened was that long stems broke off just above the roots. I tried digging it up altogether, but it was too big, at least three feet across. Frustrated, I stared angrily at the daisies. They grinned back at me triumphantly.

I left them where they were and turned my attention to the other overgrown perennials. I spared the gladioli because they were my favourites, and I hadn't the heart to touch the irises or aquilegia because they looked so delicate and vulnerable. Although the lilies-of-the-valley had spread all along the edge of the bed, I left them alone: their fragrance was so delicious that I couldn't bear to disturb them. I looked round for other victims. The showy, blowsy flowers of the peonies were short-lived, blooming only for a few, fleeting days in late spring. Their leaves alone were boring, and they occupied too much space. Clearly this plant wasn't justifying its existence. The globe thistles were too bold, too robust, with their spiky blue flower heads. They would have to go. So, too, would the rudbeckia. Its large yellow flowers pointed backwards instead of up, which I found vaguely unsettling. It looked raggedy and uneven. I had never liked it, although my mother was fond of it, for some reason.

All these hapless plants received the same treatment as the Michaelmas-daisies. Some broke off in my hands, others I dug up altogether by mistake, then tried frantically to divide where they lay on the soil, cutting between the roots with some rusty shears while the long-suffering plants wilted in the hot sunshine. I did succeed in separating a few roots, which I marched down to the wild boggy area and planted – they languished forlornly for a day or two before giving up the ghost. The other roots I tried to replant in their original spots, but they kept keeling over, because I hadn't re-dug their holes deep enough. By the time I'd done this, and remembered to water the holes, the poor plants had turned their faces to the soil: only the hardiest ones ever picked up again. A few weeks later, my mother discovered the fate of the rudbeckia. With tears in her eyes, she informed me that it had been planted to honour my middle sister's birth. Its common name was black-eyed Susan.

In spite of these dismal failures, I never gave up. I was learning all the time. The following spring, I decided that the old perennials – the few that had survived my ravages

– needed new companions. I bought seeds – marigolds, night-scented stocks, phlox, mesembryanthemums – not just because their pictures looked so glorious on the packet, but because I loved the sounds of their names, savouring them on my tongue like sweeties. I knew by now which plants liked sun. The central bed was the sunniest in the garden, so I was sure they would do well, once they'd survived the first hurdle – the sowing.

I was determined to get everything right this time. I pored over the instructions, observing and obeying them as if they were written on tablets of stone. 'Rake the soil to a fine tilth'; 'Plant at a depth of a quarter of an inch'; 'Allow half an inch between each seed'. I ran inside for my ruler, stuck it into the soil, then measured all along the row, marking off half-inches with matchsticks. I remembered to water the little holes, before and after sowing. To my amazement, they all germinated and grew – tiny islands of colour amid the well-established plants. Here, at last, was something that I'd achieved all on my own. The results were tangible and easily measurable – not like boring school work, which seemed to me a very hit-or-miss affair when it came to measuring success.

My mother was mildly encouraging of my new gardening zeal, but neither of my parents was as ecstatic as I'd hoped. They were both often preoccupied with their own concerns. Or maybe they worried that by spending hours in the garden, I was neglecting my lessons – I was a poor scholar. It is even possible that my mother secretly envied me, and wished she could be in my shoes, with her hands in the soil, crouching down in her precious plants.

I got collywobbles in my tummy just thinking about her allergy. It was ever present, waiting just below the surface of her skin. Now and then it would erupt in a milder form, probably due to one of the household irritants – bleach, washing powder, Vim, she was never sure which. Then the old rash would reappear on the palms of her hands. For a week or two they would itch like mad and once again the house would reek of calamine lotion. But compared to the serious attack of a few years earlier, this was nothing. Even so, each time it happened, I held my breath, waiting for the worst.

I was getting older, and it seemed doubly important that I took on the role of family gardener, to save my mother from herself. At this stage, we were almost sure that primulas were the culprits. I was determined not to let her near them. I could never relax if she was out in the garden, because by now I'd experienced for myself how addictive gardening was. I knew that even if she started doing something innocuous, such as deadheading roses, she'd soon be in full flow, and she wouldn't wear gardening gloves. I can sympathise. I have never worn gloves, either, and would rather have permanently toughened skin and dirty fingernails than feel a barrier between my hands and the good earth.

It is a testament to my mother's love of her garden that she still did whatever she could, whenever she could. Once, I came home from school to find her gathering fallen rose petals. Mystified, I asked her what she was up to. Her eyes sparkled as told me she was going to make rose-petal jam. For the rest of the afternoon and the entire evening, the kitchen was filled with steam, as all the available cooking pots were put to use and a thousand jam jars were sterilised. Then after a complicated process involving about a ton of petals, the jars filled up with purply-brown goo.

'Taste it!' said my mother, offering me a spoonful.

I did. It was revolting. It tasted like sugary soap. Just the scent of it put me off. I preferred rose petals in their proper place – on the roses. But I hadn't the heart to tell her, and dutifully forced it down. I felt like those visitors to Bedouin tribes that I'd heard about, who out of politeness to their hosts, swallowed whole sheep's eyes. Years later, dozens of those jam-filled jars still lined the top shelf of our larder. Maybe they improved with age, like old wine. I never had the courage to find out.

My new passion didn't stop at sowing seeds, thinning out and weeding. I was getting more ambitious. The path leading up to the air-raid shelter, originally concrete paving slabs, was even more cracked and overgrown with weeds than it had been three years ago. I'd spent a few frantic hours trying to dig out the dandelions from between the cracks, but it was a thankless task – the roots were too deep. The only solution was to lay a new path. One Saturday morning, I started levering up all the slabs with a spade and piling them up on one side. Then I got to work on the weeds, digging them all out. I had no plan in mind. I just wanted things to be under control and neat, for once. Most of my friends had neat gardens, with salvia, alyssum and lobelia standing prim and patriotic in their ordered sequences of red, white and blue, with not a single weed in sight. My own garden was wild in comparison.

By the evening, where there'd been a broken, weedy path, there now stretched a long strip of bare earth. And I hadn't given any thought to which materials would best replace the old paving slabs. When I staggered indoors in the failing light, my parents looked at me in bemused wonder, tinged with nervousness. This latest onslaught on the garden path left them baffled and slightly alarmed. Both of them preferred things left as they were. In digging up the path, I'd gone way beyond the call of duty. In their eyes, it smacked faintly of insanity.

Most parents would have suggested that we go immediately to the nearest builders' merchants for some new paving stones. In which case, I would have been encouraged to carry on with my project. Or, in view of my father's physical limitations, my mother would have been quite justified in insisting that they 'get a man in'. For some reason, neither of these things happened. I can't remember whether they were just too busy, or perhaps they weren't interested. What I do remember is the rain that fell in great torrents that evening and all night through. The next day, Sunday, the path was a quagmire. Plainly, there was nothing I could do until it dried out again. Monday was school. I had homework. So it went on for the rest of the week. Two weeks later, it would be Sports Day. I was busy practising my gymnastics routine on the lawn every spare moment. The path was forgotten. We got used to the mud after a while.

It remained that way until, a few weeks later, in the absence of any ideas from my parents, I had the urge to put all the old slabs back in a crazy-paving style, filling the gaps with gravel and beach stones. My new path didn't quite reach the air-raid shelter, which during the past three years had caved in, covering the steps with a mass of soil and rubble that had spilled onto the two remaining concrete slabs. I cleared it with a spade, and stood up to stretch my back with a sigh of satisfaction at a job well done. Speculatively, I gazed down the earth-covered steps. What a waste! There was a whole room below there, sitting idle and neglected. Surely it could be put to good use? If I could clear a passage down to the entrance, I might convert it into my own private retreat.

First, I needed to clear the steps. This in itself would be a monumental task. The concrete walls had collapsed in great blocks, which were impossible to lift. I would have to break them up. I found a hammer and chisel. Somehow, I borrowed a crowbar and pickaxe from a gullible neighbour, telling him that my father needed them urgently. I kept going for several weeks, on and off. My body ached all the time. I felt like the female Russian hammer-throwers who had begun to appear on television. They were built like tanks and looked like men. I didn't want to look like them, but I needed their strength.

At last, I managed to clear a passage down to the entrance. I hadn't been down there for years. Fear still lurked in the darkness, making me shudder – I half expected to see skeletons lying on the bunk beds. The old wooden door creaked open. The light bulb still worked. The place looked exactly as it had before, the dusty bunk beds festooned with filmy tendrils of spiders' webs, and damp patches covering the ceiling and walls. And, still stuck fast to the rough surface, was a colony of snails. There were dozens of them, huddled together – mums and dads and babies. Surely they couldn't be the same ones I'd seen three years ago? I had no idea how long snails lived. Their presence down there seemed to explain why my garden looked so underpopulated with snails. They had been hiding in the bomb shelter. I had been searching in the wrong place, among the roses and perennials. While weeding, I had vaguely noticed several craftily nibbled lupin petals, but these plants were so healthy and luxuriant that the connection between snails and lupins had not really registered. I realised that for years, the snails that had once so intrigued me had been completely out of my sight.

As I gazed at them, sleeping so peacefully, it was like meeting old friends again. Once more, I was glad of their company; once more, I stroked their shells, feeling the spiralled whorls beneath my fingertip. I wondered whether these snails were relatives of the dozens I'd almost bashed to pieces when I was breaking up the concrete. During the previous fortnight, there had been a heatwave, and just in time I'd spotted them asleep, hidden deep in the crevices. They had been stuck fast to the rubble, covered by earth. There, in the shelter, I unstuck one and turned it over. The lip of its shell was sealed up with a delicate film. I tried to replace the snail on the wall. It fell to the ground with a thump. I hadn't the heart to unstick the other poor creatures from their resting places on the walls and ceiling. This was their home, and I hadn't even decided what use I was going to put it to.

I gazed round the tiny cell. The iron bunk beds took up half the space, but the floor was dry, and the whole structure was sound. What fun it would be to convert it into my own little den, where no one would bother me, and I could make up stories to my heart's content without anyone telling me to do things, such as homework or minding my younger sisters. If I could keep it a secret, I would be able to disappear down here without being found. I was now fourteen, almost grown up. Surely I was entitled to some private space? But somehow the word 'den' wasn't right. Dens were cosy and comfortable; this place was cold and damp. And very dark, if I turned the light off. With mounting excitement, I remembered my recently discovered heroine, Marie Curie. I had a brainwave. I would turn the shelter into a laboratory!

At school, most of the time I went round in a dreamy fog of non-attention, missing half of what the teachers said. My brain seemed perpetually frozen, not at all fit for the purposes of algebra and fractions. I'd fly off into my own secret world of fantasy and stories, relying on friends to nudge me back to reality when it came to homework instructions or answering questions in class. Yet now and again, something percolated through the fuzzy layers of my consciousness and really fired me up. In English, we'd been reading *The Radium Woman, A Life of Marie Curie* by Eleanor Doorly. I found it electrifying.

Marie Curie was clever. She had a double master's degree and a fellowship and had written a thesis on the magnetisation of tempered steel. But, as if this wasn't enough, she wanted the title of Doctor. To win that, she had to discover something that had never been discovered before. Previously, a French professor called Becquerel had been studying a rare metal called uranium. He'd found something surprising and puzzling: the salts of uranium gave off rays without any contact with light. These rays were spontaneously light-giving. Marie had found an extraordinary quest for her doctorate. She was going to explain this strange radiation – where it came from and what caused it.

To do this, she studied minerals containing uranium and discovered that some were more radioactive than the uranium itself. There was only one explanation: the minerals must contain another, unknown, element. Joined by her husband, Pierre, Marie began studying a uranium ore called pitchblende, breaking it up to measure the radioactivity of each separate element. The pair discovered the existence of not one, but two new elements: polonium – named after Marie's native Poland – and radium.

Radium had a name, but Marie had not yet seen it. She had to hold it, to weigh it, before the scientists would believe her. To collect enough of the mysterious substance to be seen with the naked eye, she and Pierre would need a hundred tons of pitchblende. They spent their life savings transporting trucks full of radioactive brown dust – a waste product of uranium extraction for glass-making – from the pine forests of Bohemia to Paris. By now, Marie had a baby. But she worked long into the night inside her dark, makeshift shed, lifting huge heaps of dust into a cauldron and stirring it down, always seeking that elusive spark. It was heavy work. Sometimes she got no sleep at all. But she never, ever gave up. In the end, after four years of non-stop labour, she found her tiny glow of light and gave it to the world. Because of her discovery, radiotherapy used in the treatment of tumours has saved or prolonged many lives.

Her story sent tingles down my spine. What determination, what brilliance! What was more amazing was that I'd understood and enjoyed the science. So much so, that I was fired with my own ambition. I, too, would discover radium – well, rediscover it. I would be as single-minded, hard-working and painstaking as Marie Curie. Here was my laboratory. The black cave of the air-raid shelter was perfect. A dark place was necessary in order to find radium: otherwise I wouldn't see the spark. Marie Curie worked at night. My shelter just needed a little work on it. If I left the door wide open, any fumes would escape, and I could probably do my experiments in secret. Pitchblende was a bit more of a problem. Bohemia, where the Curies obtained their supply, was a long way away. But there was plenty of anthracite in the coal bunker, and I reckoned that if I bashed it into dust with a mallet and mixed it with some smashed-up concrete – in which I could see tiny particles sparkling – it would make a good substitute. I might even find a totally new element. Then, I'd be the school heroine. I might even get the school science prize.

In my excitement, I forgot that I wasn't doing science at school. That year, we had been made to choose between chemistry and cookery, and between physics and art. The school timetable didn't allow for all these subjects to be covered. I was hopeless at maths, and knew that there was a lot of maths in physics, so that was out. I had tried chemistry for a week, but the teacher was a disaster. We spent the first two lessons repeating, in a sing-song voice, all the formulae of all the elements in the periodic table. I hadn't a clue what an element was – the teacher hadn't bothered to explain. I had been totally out of my depth and bored out of my mind. Worse, coming out of school after these lessons, I'd met classmates carrying baskets full of cheese scones and jam tarts and fairy cakes straight from the oven, which they were busy stuffing into their mouths. There was no contest. I'd switched to cookery.

Now it was different. Marie Curie had inspired me. I set to with a will, sweeping the floor and dusting the iron bunk beds. My mind was racing with plans. I'd need a cauldron in which to boil down the anthracite and concrete dust – my own home-grown pitchblende. There was an old galvanised iron container, with handles, in the garage somewhere. It had probably been used for washing clothes in the olden days, when my mother was a girl. That would do perfectly. Then I would need to light a fire under the cauldron to heat the dust, before I could even begin to stir it with my long iron rod and render it down. I would have to use more anthracite for this purpose. It never occurred to me that this was absurd, because there was a more pressing problem. In order to heat our domestic hot water, our stove was fed with anthracite continually. It gobbled bucketfuls each day. Yet I needed it for my experiments. I imagined my mother's alarmed expression when she noticed the rapidly depleting store of coal in the bunker.

In the end, the problem resolved itself, but not in a way I'd anticipated. For some reason, the usual fortnightly delivery of coal never arrived. We were so low on anthracite that we had to heat up pans of hot water on the gas stove for washing dishes and ourselves. There certainly wasn't any to spare.

So I abandoned the idea altogether, with – although I never admitted it to myself – enormous relief. The whole thing had got too big for me. I could see that it was one of the craziest ideas I'd ever had. But, in retrospect, I realise that it was the *process* that had been so important. Learning about radium, grappling with problems – all this had been totally absorbing. Something new had stirred in me: a fascination with science. I hadn't found radium, but a different spark had been ignited. Over the years, whenever I heard about some new scientific discovery, or strange phenomenon in nature, the spark would flare up, firing my interest again. Then I'd remember Marie Curie and her extraordinary life, and how, one memorable summer, she'd inspired me to reach out far beyond myself, to a different world.

One day, I found another colony of snails. I'd been disgustedly poking round in the primulas at the base of the air-raid shelter's grassy mound, wondering whether to sneakily dig up the flowers and chuck them over the neighbour's fence. I was still worried that my mother would, next spring, forget all her good resolutions and pick a bunch to brighten the kitchen. I peered at them more closely. Many petals had been broken off; the leaves had huge holes and were wilting where they'd broken away just above the soil. Nestling among the leaves, huddled together, was a group of speckled snails just like those that I had found in the darkness below. They had identical bodies and shells, with the same brown markings. I wondered whether they were all related to one another in some way, as cousins, uncles, grandparents. Or were they separate tribes, each living in their own little encampments? Perhaps they visited one another from time to time, in the same way that I'd go to tea with school friends who lived outside Watford. If so, I wondered whether they'd find their way home again. It was a long journey, from the flowers down into the shelter, and I wondered if they could make it. Then, they'd have to go back again, or stay the night. I began to suspect that for years they had been leading a blissful life here, with a continual food supply and plenty of shade. I couldn't think how I had managed to miss them, and all the damage they had done.

I picked one up by its shell. Immediately it retracted its tentacles and disappeared inside its house. I put it down beside its companions. They seemed so happy among the primulas, and if they ate every last scrap, well, good luck to them. My mother would be spared temptation, and there were plenty of other flowers for her to pick when springtime came round again.

Now I had found three colonies of snails – in the rubble, in the shelter and in the primulas. This lot seemed happily settled in their home. I was intrigued by their need to be so close together. Other species of snail that I had noticed while visiting the gardens of school friends seemed to lead much more solitary lives.

On impulse, I gathered a few of them together. Gently, I set them down on the path. I lined them up at the edge of a stone slab. Then I watched as they began their jagged trajectory towards the opposite edge. The concrete was rough and dry. The snails weren't at all happy. They stood still and waved their tentacles about as if trying to reorient themselves. They reminded me of blind people tap-tapping white sticks along the pavement. Some snails stopped and went on strike, curling themselves up in their shells. The more determined ones streaked across at a fair pace, tempting others to leap cannily onto their slime trails for an easier ride. The leaders were making straight for the primulas. They seemed to know where home was. As I watched their progress across the difficult terrain, I wondered how fast they were moving.

I had heard about the amazing speeds of cheetahs and other fleet-footed animals. My snails were right at the other end of the spectrum, I reckoned. Yet those front-runners, in their homing race back to the primulas, had been going at a cracking pace. It would be fun to time them with a stopwatch and a measuring stick. A few of my racing snails were still on strike. I debated whether to leave them where they were. Then, as if in answer to my thoughts, I heard a fluty call. A blackbird had flown down into the peach tree. Soon, it was joined by a couple of its mates. They stared down at my snails. That settled it. I picked the creatures up and put them back safely in the primulas.

My garden continued to be a source of learning. Gradually, I was becoming aware that everything in and around it connected up in some way. Some of this was obvious: the plants needed air and sunlight and water. We'd just learnt about photosynthesis in biology, and for the first time, this subject came alive for me. But this connectedness revealed itself in other, stranger ways. Each morning, while I was getting dressed, I could hear a tapping sound under my window. When I looked out, there'd be a thrush, cracking a snail shell against a stone, using it as an anvil. Always the same stone – and I swear it was the same thrush. There was something about the vigorous way it jerked its beak. So the snails in my garden were breakfast for thrushes. It wasn't ideal for the snails, but this was nature, working as it should.

My mother unwittingly helped in all this. Every morning, she'd open the back door and fling out stale bread from the bread bin. Huge flocks of birds would swoop down onto the lawn: chaffinches, blackbirds, timid sparrows and tits, aggressive starlings, and thrushes, dozens of thrushes. So my mother also was part of this wholeness. I hadn't yet heard the word 'ecosystem', but at fourteen I knew that my garden was a whole, living being with its own heartbeat. I could feel it pulse and throb inside me, too.

Very occasionally – and I could never make it happen, much as I tried – I'd experience something deeply strange as I planted and weeded, or stood on the lawn in the stillness of early evening, watching the sunset. It always started with an odd, spellbound silence. Tiny electric tingles would prickle my neck, and goosebumps appeared all over my arms. Then, suddenly, everything – the garden, the birds, the trees – would stand still, as if a camera shutter had clicked in my brain. The garden seemed to be holding its breath, while I – the consciousness that was me – expanded into every corner. It was a moment of pure radiance. I called it catching myself alive.

FOUR

Grand Designs

I n 1962, my student days were over. I was back living in Watford and working in London. I enjoyed the leisurely train journey up to Baker Street on the Metropolitan Line. Croxley, Moor Park, Northwood, Northwood Hills, Pinner . . . I could have recited all the stops in my sleep. Lulled by the clackety-clack of the wheels as the train rattled along, I would gaze down at the gardens bordering the track. I marvelled at the variety of patterns that could be imposed on the same simple shape: a long, narrow strip running down from house to railway line. It was a brief glimpse into the tastes, priorities and even characters of people I had never met. Tidy gardens with mown lawns and bright flower borders; gardens given over to vegetable plots; chaotic spaces littered with rusty bedsteads and broken bicycles. Some people clearly hated the whole business and had concreted the lot, while other gardens were children's paradises with slides, swings, climbing frames, play tents and paddling pools.

Many happy commuting hours would pass as I conjured up my own perfect garden. 'Garden' was too humble a term to describe my imaginary parkland, with its swathes of lawn sweeping down towards the sea from a manor house with mullioned windows and ornate chimneys. I'd spend my days in the shell grotto, from where I would direct my team of gardeners. The orchard, protected from neighbouring farmland by a ha-ha, would be famous in gardening circles for its hundred varieties of local fruit. Pineapples would grow in deep pits in specialised Victorian hot frames, while a walled garden would provide all my vegetables. Best of all were the trees. A European larch would grace the lawn, surrounded by a few cedars-of-Lebanon and many oaks. From the high vantage point of my bedroom window all this splendour would stretch into the distance until, beyond the mighty stature of the trees, there would shimmer an emerald sea.

But, as my granny used to say, one must cut one's cloth according to one's purse (or something like that, anyway). The contrast between the garden of my dreams and the reality of my first garden could not have been greater.

The curious grunting was getting louder. Sounding alarmingly near, it roused me from my hot, sticky slumber. My heart thudding, I propped myself up on one elbow. My children, Matthew, aged six, and Sarah, four and a half, were sleeping peacefully on mattresses laid out on the grass, blissfully unaware that there was a monster prowling round the garden. I glanced across to the camp bed next to mine, where my husband, Dan, was sitting up, his face a study in martyred long-suffering mixed with terror.

'Whose idea was this?' he asked, tersely. 'I have to go to work tomorrow.'

Without waiting for an answer, he untangled himself from the white sheet that covered him like a shroud and bounded back into the house.

I could hardly blame him. Sleeping under the stars on this sweltering night in 1976 had seemed a good idea at the time. In the hottest, driest summer on record for many years, the heat and stuffiness in our bedrooms was unbearable. So, at my suggestion, after bathing the children in the government's new regulation five inches of water, just before dusk we dragged the mattresses and camp beds out to the back lawn. The children thought it a great adventure, but for my husband, nothing was as good as his own bed.

I sat up and looked about. The sounds were coming from the nearby compost heap. Four round and dark and extremely spiky creatures suddenly emerged and, in a determined line, scuttled past my bed and across the lawn. They disappeared into the bushes in the far corner of the garden, still snuffling. The 'tu-whit' of a tawny owl and the answering 'tu-whoo' were so close that I was disappointed not to catch a glimpse of them as they suddenly swooped down behind some trees. Moths brushed my face and, flying under the eaves of next-door's roof, I could see the outline of dozens of pipistrelle bats.

I had never in my life been so close to the creatures of the night. It felt special, a privilege. I lay down again, with a contented sigh, revelling in the heightened atmosphere.

Now all sounds seemed magnified, every creak and whisper of twigs and leaves, the faint scuttling of a mouse or shrew. I could almost hear the plants transpiring. The distant bark of a dog was so sudden that I jumped, my heart thumping.

Matthew and Sarah had woken up and were staring, entranced, at a shooting star. Together we watched the streak of light slowly travel across the midnight-blue darkness, before it was hidden behind the rooftops. Gradually I drifted off to sleep again, waking just before dawn with soaking wet hair and a soggy sheet that clung clammily to my shoulders. Even so, there was something magical about the silence of that pre-dawn hour. The lawn glistened, every blade of grass sheathed in a silver shard of sparkling dew. The birds were still asleep, and the hedgehogs had scarpered to pastures new.

By eleven o'clock that morning, the temperature had risen to eighty degrees and was getting hotter by the minute. The grass had resumed its sickly, yellowish tinge. My runner beans had mostly given up, their withered stems strewn along the ground. The thirsty hydrangea's electric-blue flowers were now a washed-out pink. The annuals that I had so hopefully planted at the end of May had brown edges to the petals and yellowing leaves. Even the apple tree in the centre of the lawn looked parched and dry, with leaves that turned to powder when I touched them and baby apples that fell to the ground.

Huge areas of southern England, including our Surrey garden, had turned into desert.

Four and a half years ago, when we moved here with a toddler and a new baby on the way, I had accepted that I would never own a manor house. I would have to make the best of this garden, with all its limitations. Although it was quite a decent size, roughly thirty feet long and fifty feet wide, the raw material was not promising. It was a boring rectangle, twice as wide as long, with no curves or kinks. Borders ran along the bottom and right-hand fences, planted with shrubs. The bumpy lawn was great for space-hopping but a nightmare for my husband to mow. There had been a greenhouse once, which had been removed by the previous owners, leaving a broken, unusable square of concrete. But the garden's worst attributes were not its own fault. Our property was not, to put it mildly, situated in the best position. The main road outside our front gate was getting busier by the minute, being one of the most direct routes up to London. Lorries rattled by, all day long and half the night. I hated working in the front garden because of the constant racket and petrol fumes.

For logistical and financial reasons we were stuck here, and destined to stay for the foreseeable future. So, until our fortunes changed, I longed to do something with this garden, to make it special. Even though it lacked distinction, it did have two very attractive features. In the middle of the lawn was an apple tree with the most unusual and tasty apples. They were sweet cookers, or tart eaters, depending on one's preference. Large and rounded, green and smooth, they burst into crimson colour as soon as they were ripe. Wrapped individually in newspaper, they stored well in our cool garage over the winter. My family had to suffer months of apple pies and apple crumbles, and I gave loads away. Later, I found out that they were called 'Charles Ross', but I have never encountered them since.

Nearby, with its roots in the lawn, grew an ancient, free-standing wisteria tree. Its trunk and branches were all intertwined, as gnarled and knobbly as the limbs of Father Time. The land on which our property stood had once belonged to a small manor house, and had been divided up into several small plots, including ours. On top of the front gateposts were two imposing concrete balls, a legacy of its former grandeur. They say that we should be careful what we wish for. Someone in the universe's department of wishes had obviously picked up on the 'manor house' part of my fantasy, and completely ignored the rest. But as a tiny reminder of what might have been, the wisteria had stayed, delighting us with its graceful lilac pendants.

It was plain that the garden was set in its ways and would remain always so. But I was impatient to make my mark. I decided that it needed an outstanding feature, a focus to draw the eye. We discovered Wisley, the garden of the Royal Horticultural Society. It was just a short drive away along the M25, and an ideal place for the children to toddle about while I honed my grand designs. I was particularly impressed with the rockery. Climbing its winding paths, among massive rocks and tumbling alpines that I had never seen before, was like taking a walk in the Swiss Alps. There were varieties within varieties, such as the sedums, which curled into nooks and crannies. Thick cushions of rock-rose and carpets of gypsophila cascaded over the boulders, which looked as if they had been there since the dawn of time. A rockery, I decided, would give my garden some pizzazz. I would make my rockery a tiny version of Wisley's, planting as many varieties of alpines as I could into the available space. But, during the first year in our new home, because of the constant demands of baby feeds and nappy changes, I could do little more than throw a few rocks into a higgledy-piggledy pattern.

Nineteen seventy-six was to be The Year of the Garden. The previous year, with the children older and more independent, I should, in theory, have had more time for gardening. But we'd begun a two-storey extension, which took over our lives completely. The back lawn sank into a lake of mud while soakaways were dug. Every spare bit of ground was a repository for bricks, breeze blocks, roof trusses and huge heaps of sand and cement.

When at last, the following year, it was all finished, I gazed out of my bedroom window one fine morning at a garden that looked unexpectedly bereft. The ugly, inconvenient obstacles of the building works had become part of the scene. Grass, dandelions and ferns had sprung up between the stacks of bricks and piles of cement, creating a sculptured, surreal landscape. I could have entered it in the Chelsea Flower Show: entitled The Builder's Garden, with a couple of breeze-block seats and a summer house suspended from a crane, it would easily have won a prize. Now that everything had been cleared away, all I could see were crushed shrubs, borders choked with bindweed and ivy, and bare, sandy earth instead of a lawn. Empty and sad, the garden cried out for care.

I set to, clearing, weeding, pruning and digging out a small vegetable plot. I felt the thrill of imposing my stamp on what was, in effect, virgin land. My husband left me mainly to my own devices. Now and then, at weekends, he would emerge from the safety of the house, blinking like a mole in the bright sunlight, and offer welcome cups of tea.

May was the start of the hot weather. The children loved it. Out came the paddling pool and the play tent. We dug out a sandpit. The garden was their playground, reminding me of my own childhood. One of my most treasured photos is of the children jumping in and out of the paddling pool while soaking one another with the hose. The photo, taken with our new Polaroid camera, which miraculously churned out an instant snap, has that 1970s look – the reds and greens are exaggerated and the definition is poor. Yet it highlights the excitement on the children's faces, the joy of rapid movement captured for ever in the misty stream of water, a few beautifully delineated, separate drops escaping into the foreground.

At the end of June, temperatures soared into the nineties and the drought began with a vengeance, sapping every ounce of our energy. We moved slowly, languorously, punctuating the days with icy drinks and cold showers. The car stickers that exhorted us to 'Have a Bath with a Friend' did not suggest how to rescue our gardens: the sun-scorched earth was as cracked and dry as an Indian river delta before the rains. Gardening became an activity of the past. Hot sticky evenings meant that, once the children were in bed, my efforts were concentrated on saving my favourite plants, mostly vegetables. With a hosepipe ban in force, it was a matter of filling up watering cans over and over again.

My rockery was still in a rough state. Late one afternoon, clouds appeared unexpectedly in the sky, with a light breeze. The delight of feeling cool sent me into a fury of gardening activity. I started to move the stones and arrange them more artistically. I cleared away the smaller ones from the edges, then reached into the middle for a real humdinger of a rock, at least a foot across, half-buried under the soil. It was too heavy to lift, so I dragged it towards me. There was a nasty crunch.

I lifted one end of the boulder. The crunch had come from the desiccated remains of a colony of garden snails as I'd cracked their shells. Most were still intact, but they were dead. Their pale, almost white shells, as delicate and transparent as pieces of porcelain, massed together as if in a communal grave. As I looked down at the ghostly forms of my childhood companions, long-buried memories surfaced, of snail races, and of snail colonies hiding in the air-raid shelter in my parents' garden. I picked one up and peered inside the shell cavity. Its inhabitant had long departed to the great lupin patch in the sky. The shell felt rough, and all the zigzags and speckles had eroded. But a few of the other shells had lost colour only on their apex. The markings were paler, but still evident.

All the wildlife had suffered in the drought. Worms and slow-worms had dried out, lying on the surface of grass and soil. Hungry birds pecked disconsolately around what had once been the lawn. Even the bees seemed fed up, their buzzing muted as they landed on shrivelled blooms. It was hardly surprising that the snails had perished.

I poked round a bit more, digging deeper into the soil. Here were more snails. They were dead, too. The soil, though dry, was cool, yet their shells were white and partially eroded. This didn't make sense – surely the snails would have been more protected down below? Puzzled, I investigated other areas in the garden, particularly the dampest part near the children's paddling pool, which we always left filled with water. Disgusting though it was by evening, full of the drowned corpses of bluebottles and mosquitoes, any sensible mollusc would surely make a snail-line for the pool and take up permanent residence nearby. Sure enough, a few snails were huddled beneath the plastic, taking huge draughts of liquid like the thirsty punters at the pub over the road. I dug about under some flowerpots and found more snails curled up. Their shells, too, were faded, and I feared that they were as dead as their cousins in the rockery. Then they stretched out their tentacles and glared at me.

Close by, the builders had left a pile of bricks against the wall of the new extension, coated with a thin sprinkling of white, like a cake dusted with icing sugar. Several snails were clinging to the wall. Why, I wondered, would they want to be up there when they could be out foraging? Under the brick pile were more sleepy snails, but this at least made sense, because the ground beneath the bricks was visibly damp. Yet their shells looked weather-beaten. I tried to prise one away, but it refused to budge.

I walked across the lawn in my bare feet, relishing the soft coolness of the dewy evening grass. Yet there was also an unpleasant scratchiness between my toes. I looked down and noticed that between every blade of grass was a thin scattering of builders' sand. For a whole year there had been a mountain of the stuff in the middle of the lawn, and its residue lingered. The children's favourite occupation of chucking their play sand out of the pit as far as they could throw it must have made an even rougher passage for the snails as they slimed across the lawn in search of food and shelter.

It was almost dark – too late to do any more work. I sat in the middle of the sandpit, swishing the sand round thoughtfully. Why were some shells intact and vivid, while others had faded into washed-out replicas of their former selves?

Some people have dedicated their lives to these questions. I decided to dip my toe into their science – conchology, the study of mollusc shells – and borrow some books from the library. I discovered that snail shells come in an astonishing variety of patterns and shapes. They can be cone-shaped or flat; smooth or deeply grooved; many-whorled or not whorled at all. In Britain, their colours range from creamy white to brown, with all the shades in between. Some are yellow or yellow-green or orange. One snail has regular reddish-brown stripes; others are covered with tiny hairs.

British snails

Truncatellina claustralis (1.5–1.8mm).

Discus rotundatus (5.5–7mm).

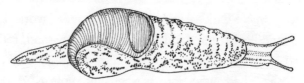

Semilaxis pyrenaicus (5–6mm).

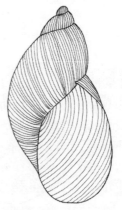

Cernuella virgata (8–25mm).

Succinea putris (10–17mm).

Cepaea hortensis (14–20mm).

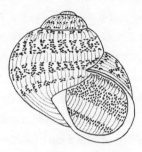

Cornu aspersum (25–35mm).

Cepaea nemoralis (12 –22mm).

Helix pomatia (30–50mm).

My brown, speckled snails were garden snails, *Cornu aspersum* (*cornu* is Latin for 'horn'; *aspersum* means 'scattered'). Until recently, they were known as *Helix aspersa* (*helix* is Greek for 'spiral'). Their shells are made up of two separate layers: the inner ostracum and the outer periostracum. The main building block of the ostracum is calcium carbonate (chalk), which snails need to maintain the strength and solidity of their shells – they do better on lime-rich, alkaline soils. It is also the main ingredient of cement. The snails in my Surrey garden, which seemed to have such a mysterious fetish for builders' rubble, were desperate to top up their lime.

The periostracum covers the surface of the shell. It is a horny layer, composed of an organic protein called conchiolin, which coats the ostracum like varnish on wood, making it shiny and smooth and heightening its markings and colours – which range from cream through ochre and tan to various shades of brown. This artistic, finishing touch on top of the ostracum helps to give each species its distinctive appearance. The periostracum is vital to the healthy maintenance of the shell. It can be easily worn away. Snails that live near beaches, where the constant abrasion of the sand erodes the outer layer, have a bare, mottled appearance, like that of newly plastered walls with the first thin coat of white paint applied. Dead snails lose their periostracum much more rapidly as they lie exposed to sun, wind and rain. This explained the white shells of the dead snails I had seen in my rockery. Whether or not the drought had caused their deaths was unclear.

The shell is crucial to the snail's survival. It protects the internal organs and provides shelter into which it can withdraw when it senses danger. I cringe when I remember how my friend and I made their lives a nightmare with our unintentionally cruel games – poking different bits of their bodies and chuckling delightedly as they disappeared into their houses. The shell also preserves moisture. The snail has a very thin, soft skin, from which it secretes slime through many glands. In dry conditions, this mucus – so essential for movement – dries out. So the snail survives by withdrawing into its shell, and for added protection it draws a membrane, like a film of Sellotape, over the shell's mouth.

Baby snails emerge from their eggs with fully formed shells, but these are thin and transparent. As they grow, they thicken and harden, adding more whorls. But this doesn't happen in neat, annual increments, as we had believed when we were children. Growth can speed up, or slow down. In winter, or during a drought, it might stop altogether for a while.

I had always thought of the snail's shell as its ultimate protection – its safe house. But 'safe as houses' is no such thing when the weather unleashes its extremes. Not just for snails, but for humans, too – as I was to find out a few years later.

FIVE

Tempest and Shelter

he weatherman looked relaxed as he predicted that the next day or two would be windy, with some heavy rain. He even smiled as he said: 'Earlier on today, apparently, a woman rang the BBC and said she heard that there was a hurricane on the way; well, if you're watching, don't worry, there isn't, but having said that, actually, the weather will become very windy, but most of the strong winds, incidentally, will be down over Spain and across into France.'

Busy writing a shopping list and trying to pair up my children's socks from the mountain of clothes in the linen basket, I barely took notice of the forecast. The afternoon of 15 October 1987 had been pleasantly refreshing as I forked over the vegetable patch, ready for the autumn frosts to break down the large clods of earth. While I dug, my mind raced ahead to tomorrow's gardening plans. I would buy some seeds – broad beans for nitrogen fixing, lettuces and tomatoes. Now was the time to plant raspberry canes.

Oh, and some hellebores would really brighten up the border on a dismal February day.

The garden was taking shape at last. It was never going to be the garden of my dreams, but I was learning to work within its limitations. A recently built patio wound round the back of the house. New fuchsias, chrysanthemums and late-flowering dahlias mingled with the shrubs in the borders, and my rockery sprouted varieties of heather that would provide colour in the winter months.

That night, I slept fitfully, periodically jolted by rattling windows and picture frames. The floor seemed to be rocking, together with the bed, as if the heavy traffic hurtling past our house was shaking it to its very foundations. I was so used to this earth-moving activity that it never alarmed me. As I tossed and turned in my sleep, one particular sound wove itself uneasily into my dreams: the constant wail of the wind. It rose and fell and rose again, to a screeching crescendo accompanied by thuds and bangs and crashes. But over the years I had trained myself to sleep through almost anything except the cry of a child.

Early the next morning, I stretched and yawned myself awake, listening for the usual traffic noises. It was so unnaturally quiet that I leapt out of bed and parted the curtains. I peered out into the pre-dawn light, trying to make sense of the strange landscape in the back garden below. Suddenly I felt myself go cold.

There was no garden. Just a strange open space connecting with other open spaces everywhere I looked. The fences of most of the surrounding properties were down, some leaning at crazy angles, others flattened on the ground. A tall tree was resting against the roof of a neighbour's house, perilously close to the upstairs windows. Our lawn had disappeared under a thick layer of debris: branches, roof tiles, twigs and uprooted plants, including the heathers from my rockery. Even in the dim light, I could see a lot of broken glass.

Dan came in with our morning cups of tea.

'It's much worse out the front,' he said. 'Trees strewn across the road and pavement. No traffic at all. God knows how I'll get to work.'

Together we stood at the window, surveying the scene below.

'Look at that!' Dan said suddenly, visibly upset. 'The wisteria's down.'

This unusual feature, the only thing of any distinction in our garden, lay across the lawn, its ancient limbs in the air surrounded by a cloak of fresh green leaves. Shocked, I gazed down at my special tree, wrenched too soon from its good life in the earth.

The children in the village, including my four-year-old son, Nathan, loved it all. That morning, as we climbed over the tree trunks obstructing the pavement, our journey to his playgroup took three times longer than usual. Most of the stately oaks that had graced the village green for centuries had fallen. Their upturned roots fanned out in massive arcs, while underneath, where the hurricane had hauled them out of the ground, cavities gaped several feet deep. I felt frightened. It seemed unbelievable that these oaks, symbols of solidity and permanence, could have been wrested so easily by the force of the gale. Later, in the news, I heard that six out of the seven oaks had fallen in the town of Sevenoaks in Kent, while Kew Gardens had lost many valuable and beautiful specimens. Winds of ninety-four miles per hour had been recorded across southern England. It was the worst tempest in England since the great storm of 1703.

During the following days, highways men came with their screeching chainsaws, slicing up the huge trunks lying on the pavement as if they were butter and loading them onto trucks to be carted away. It was heart-rending to contemplate the fate of these roadside companions, sycamores, rowans and birches that had for years provided grace and shade, as well as food and shelter for the birds.

Clearing away the damage took months. Our flattened fence had to be repaired and dragged back into place, and all the strewn branches tidied away. We couldn't bring ourselves to move the wisteria, and for weeks it lay across the grass, leaves withering, until a neighbour offered to put it on the skip that was taking away his fallen tree. We had got off lightly, with a few roof tiles missing and a chimney pot blown away. Others were not so fortunate. People sleeping in their beds had been injured by trees that had crashed right through the roof. In some cases, entire roofs had blown off. Sheds flying past windows had been reported, and there were many injuries due to shattered windows. On that dreadful night, eighteen people in England were killed.

The storm had other, surprising effects. It revealed an underground population of creatures that had been hidden from view. Beetles scuttled in the bowl of the uprooted wisteria, together with worms and slow-worms. All things that creep through the earth seemed to be promenading about the garden, finding their way round this strange new landscape.

At the beginning of October, before the storm, the slugs and snails had mostly disappeared, to my relief. They had a taste for my dahlias and chrysanthemums, and I was pleased when a cold snap sent some of them away. I knew that snails hibernated, and thought that my remaining plants would now be safe for the winter.

After the storm, however, there was a sudden snail influx. They arrived joyfully from the borderless gardens all about. My patch was now part of the Common Market, no passport needed. The snails joined the beetles and worms in exploring the garden, gleefully sniffing out late-flowering blooms and getting well and truly stuck in. In the end, I gave up chasing them, abandoning my precious blooms to their fate. In November, the first frosts attacked the remaining growth, leaving drooping brown leaves and petals. These were not good enough for the slimy gourmands, and at last they retreated.

One December day, I poked about under the fence that still lay unfixed on the ground. Wedging a couple of bricks under one corner, I levered it up and peered beneath. A large colony of snails clustered together, upside down, clinging to the wood. They looked as if they were in a hundred-year sleep. Or maybe they were dead? I unstuck one. The round opening to its shell was sealed with the Sellotape-like substance that I had seen before during very hot weather. When I prodded it, it was firm; it gave way a little, then bounced back, like healthy flesh.

The next day, while Nathan played on the village green, I inspected the upturned oaks. These massive structures were now superb climbing frames (this was before children's play became a health and safety issue). On the green, nothing had been cleared away. Great piles of leaves decayed on the ground, filling the pits beneath the upturned roots like a slippery, sludgy brown stew. It had a strong, earthy smell, not unpleasant. Many rotting logs were scattered, filled with burrowing insects. I dug underneath the logs and leaves and found more garden snails. But these were dead, and their speckled shells were white and pitted, like almond stones, with deep grooves in their rounded whorls. I guessed they hadn't been dead long, because near the mouths of their shells were the shrunken remnants of membranes. There was a mystery here. What fate had befallen these creatures while the snails in my garden had been hibernating?

The snail's epiphragm – the protective seal that covers the mouth of its shell – is, to my mind, a piece of extraordinary engineering, equal in its ingenuity to the shell itself. It is made of mucus mixed with protein, a glutinous soup strengthened by deposits of calcium carbonate – the same basic ingredient of the snail's shell. Like a good waterproof jacket, it lets air in and out, protecting the snail from rainwater while regulating the humidity inside its shell.

For extra strength, the snail can lay down several layers of epiphragm. The clever creature can adapt its thickness and structure – for example, an increase in calcium carbonate – to a variety of environmental conditions. It might become thinner or thicker, depending on the season and the temperature. A few species, including garden snails, can create a different, solid and very hard epiphragm with a higher quantity of lime. With a small perforation to allow breathing, this preserves even more moisture and body heat and protects snails from predators, such as carnivorous beetle larvae. It is a magnificent all-purpose tool for sitting out many months of hostile conditions.

The sleeping snails I had found in my garden after the Great Storm of 1987 had all manufactured an epiphragm to suit the winter weather. A cold spell had triggered their hibernation, which can last from October or November until spring, when warmth and sunshine coax them out of their resting places. As for the desiccated snails under the leaf litter in the park, their fate was not due to a faulty membrane. The decomposing leaves and roots had most likely unleashed a host of fungi, algae and bacteria, which had feasted on their flesh and eaten into their shells, exposing them to the destructive ravages of predatory creatures. Glow-worm larvae feed on snails, while fly larvae develop inside snails and their eggs, eventually killing their hosts. The molluscs' eventual demise could also have been hastened by the tannic acids found in the decaying leaf litter itself.

My garden snails had weathered the 1976 drought in the same way they survived the Great Storm. The epiphragm plays a key role in aestivation, a kind of hot-weather hibernation. During heatwaves, when the lack of food and water puts them in serious danger of drying out, the membrane conserves the moisture in their bodies. They curl up inside their shells and find a shaded crevice or flowerpot in which to shelter.

Only when weather conditions improve do the snails emerge, heading straight towards the nearest puddle to replenish their mucus. Having quenched their thirst, they must tackle their ravenous hunger. They are ready to wreak havoc in the garden.

SIX

On the Rampage

I could never understand why Adrian Mole, aged thirteen and three-quarters, was so sniffy about living in a cul-de-sac. For me, it was the next best thing to a manor house.

The acquisition of a home in a traffic-free zone, without intercontinental trucks shaking my bed and shattering my dreams, had become more than an ideal – it was an obsession. Throw in a south-facing garden, sloping downwards with enough space for a variety of features – including a pond – and I would go gratefully and contentedly to my grave.

In 1994, as a single parent, I moved to my present house in Totnes, Devon, with my young son, Nathan. This time, someone in the universe's department of wishes was in a more bountiful mood. My new garden fulfilled all my requirements, even down to a defunct but restorable pond. The house was near the end of a cul-de-sac. It was so quiet that at first I found the absence of traffic unnerving. At night, the hoot of an owl, the sigh of the breeze and the rustle of leaves stood out against the silence, amplified and finely tuned as if captured by the most sophisticated sound-recording system.

Every morning I awoke to the sound of seagulls, which I have loved since my favourite holiday by the sea when I was nine years old. Then, the screeching calls would herald the excitement of a day on the beach: learning to swim, collecting shells and the discovery of tiny shrimps and starfish in rock pools. In May 1994, for the first time in many years, I was deafened by the dawn chorus. Woven into the gulls' cacophony were the individual songs of blackbirds, chaffinches and robins, unsullied by the constant, wearying drone of traffic. Working in the garden was a delight. I could be out all day and hear nothing but the companionable, unhurried arrival of neighbours as they parked their cars. An aeroplane was an event. People came to their windows to see what this strange intrusion signified. Army helicopters were more common, but they never bothered me after the ear-splitting days of living so close to Heathrow airport.

The day after moving in, I started on the garden. Once again, there was not much scope for change. Both the front and the back gardens had been set – literally – in stone. They sloped down towards the valley, and both were landscaped on two levels. At the back, the upper, lawned area, which was retained by huge, roughly hewn square granite blocks, had an enormous central flower bed at the end of it. Below, a sloping lawn led to a row of dark conifers. The front garden also was on two levels. It supported its upper level by means of a three-foot wall made out of rocks loosely, and precariously, mortared together. It had a rockery, and a pond, which the previous owners had filled in by dumping rocks and boulders into its depths. Stonework was everywhere – and so were slugs and snails.

I had never seen so many molluscs gathered together in one small area. At the back, I found them in the cracks between the great blocks of granite. In the front garden, they hid under the retaining wall, from where they would saunter over to the rock-strewn waters of the pond as if enjoying a health spa specially laid on for their benefit. By their huge numbers and insatiable appetites, they soon made it very clear that they owned the place and that I was an interloper who had had the nerve to invade their territory.

My first actions reflected my priorities – creating a garden before sorting out the house. After unpacking the kettle and Nathan's toys, I began to clear the pond in the front garden. In doing so, I disturbed many of those settled and highly territorial creatures. When I prised them away from the damp rocks where they clung, limpet-like, they first retreated into their shells, then emerged, balefully, stretching out their tentacles. There was nowhere to put the rocks except on top of the rockery, so I heaped them, plus the snails, on top of the existing stones, creating a highly unstable pile to be attended to one day in the future. I worked for days on that pond. When I had scooped out the stinking water, I started on the sludge at the bottom, thus, in my ignorance, disturbing the habitat of a myriad pond creatures, including dragonfly and mayfly larvae. The structure had been lined with concrete and, as I was to discover later, leaked badly, but for now I cleaned the slime from the edges. Then, to compound my list of sins, I filled it to the brim with tap water.

Soon afterwards, I bought a Flowform — a wonderful arrangement of three sculptured stone basins that were set in steps sloping down from the top of the rockery to just above the edge of the pond. A pump propelled the water round in a loop: it cascaded down onto the basins, where it danced delightfully round each one in figures of eight. Eventually water boatmen, pond skaters, damselfly nymphs and newts took up residence in the pond, thanks not to me but to the plentiful Devon rain that replaced the noxious tap water.

The first February, my garden was invaded by a parade of toads. They marched up the road, turning sharp right at the end of the cul-de-sac into my front garden, where, with joyful croaks, they dived into the pond. At night, their mating calls were raucous for a couple of months, resulting in long strings of spawn that looked like necklaces of pearls, with a black blob inside each one. They clung to the rush grass, irises and mimulus at the water's edge, and later the blobs turned into tadpoles. Once, I made the mistake of turning on the pump while I was busy elsewhere in the garden. I returned a few minutes later to see a black fountain of tadpoles hurtling down the Flowform and spinning dizzily round and round the basins in perfect figures of eight. Luckily they recovered from this childhood trauma sufficiently to lose their tails and grow into miniature toads no bigger than small beetles, their tiny limbs and hands perfectly formed.

With the pond finished, it took some time to get to grips with the clay soil. In rainy periods, which happened often, the earth became so waterlogged that it was unworkable. By contrast, in long spells of hot, dry weather, it caked into clods as hard and shatterproof as the rocks on the rockery. It was also packed with small stones. Every spring, I would remove mountains of them and, by the following year, they would be back, as if returned by some malevolent spirit of the garden. My constant application of humus and compost was time-consuming and ultimately fruitless – the greedy soil gobbled up all my attempts to make it more friable.

I spent hours poring over gardening books. Clay, I discovered, was much favoured by brassicas, such as cabbage and cauliflower, and disdained by carrots. But I disliked many brassicas and loved carrots, so this was disappointing. However, runner beans and French beans seemed happy enough to put down roots in the heavy soil. With hope and great expectations, I planted these in my newly dug vegetable patch.

This was when I had my first contretemps with the snails. The previous owners of the house had not been interested in growing vegetables or flowers, so, during my first year, waves of exultant molluscs swarmed over the beans. At first, I religiously picked them off, one by one, and deposited them elsewhere in the garden, hoping they would settle there. Fat chance. By nightfall, they were back, eager and ready for their evening meal. I slung them on top of the brambly hedge at the end of the garden, several yards away, but they returned. One particular snail had unusual yellow markings throughout its shell. Regular as clockwork, it turned up for its dinner, making its leisurely way towards the same runner-bean stem night after night.

I talked to the neighbours in my road. Many of them were true Devonians with at least three generations in the graveyard. 'Aarr,' one man told me in his soft Devon burr. 'The answer lies in the soil. Heavy clay, it be. Snails love it. Tharr be something in that soil that they can't get enough of. I've known folk move right away because of it – upcountry to foreign parts like Lincolnshire.'

Clearly, I needed to find out more about soil.

While gazing out of train windows when visiting other parts of the country, I had always been struck by the different colours of the earth. In Norfolk, endless rows of cabbages grew in soil that was almost black, in contrast to the red earth of Devon. I learnt that soil's colour is influenced by its mineral content (iron in particular) and organic constituents. Iron forms secondary minerals with a yellow or red colour; manganese, sulphur and nitrogen can form black mineral deposits – hence the black loam of Norfolk; organic matter decomposes into black or brown compounds.

I found out that sixteen elements are essential for the growth and reproduction of plants: carbon, hydrogen, oxygen, phosphorus, potassium, nitrogen, sulphur, calcium, iron, magnesium, boron, manganese, copper, zinc, molybdenum and chlorine. This was impressive – I had no idea that soil was so complex. I bought a soil-testing kit to find out if my soil was acidic or limy. It came out as more lime than acid, which explained why my snails were so settled. They had a ready supply of calcium, so vital to the structure of their shells.

One of the most important elements on the list was nitrogen, which makes plants darker green and more succulent. The only storehouse of any kind is organic matter. For the good of my plants, my next job was to buy a round green plastic bin resembling a Dalek and to fill it with all my vegetable peelings.

I became a compost bore. When friends came round for a meal, they would splutter over their soup when I informed them that female urine was the best compost activator. They choked on their spaghetti as I boasted about all the worms in my bin that had appeared from nowhere while other gardeners had to buy them from specialist wormeries. As I pondered the relative merits of chicken versus pigeon droppings, they turned slightly green, finally falling asleep in their fruit salad when I told them how long a pineapple husk takes to decompose.

The good news about my heavy, sticky soil was that it had a high capacity for holding nutrients and water. Clay soils resist wind and water erosion better than silt and sandy soils because the particles are more tightly packed together. They also retain more organic material than soils without clay – proteins that normally break down readily can resist decomposition when bound to clay particles. Hence the bad news: snails were perfectly happy in my garden and would never relocate to Lincolnshire.

By the second year in my new home, relations between the snails and me had become even more strained. The front-garden snails seemed to resent having their long-established resting places disturbed. By night, they found new hiding places; by day, they found fresh plants to attack beyond the rockery. In the back garden, I had branched out into annuals and perennials, planting them in the centre of the enormous central flower bed. Mollusc-wise, this area was a nightmare. For years, snails and slugs had hidden in the surrounding stonework. These voracious creatures were not choosy, unlike the gourmand Surrey snails. The already established perennials had only just survived by the skin of their much-munched leaves, a pathetic sight. The snails would devour anything, even things that, according to my gardening manuals, they were supposed to dislike.

'You can be confident that snails and slugs will leave the following plants alone', one guide advised smugly. Most plants on such lists were colourless and tough-leaved, like mother-in-law's tongue. But I craved a garden that would delight my eyes with its vibrant explosions of colour. The snails had not read the literature. When I planted campanulas, in which they were supposed to have no interest, the gluttons fell upon their soft, bell-shaped petals like addicts offered their favourite fix. Within a day the plants had been razed to the ground.

One manual said that snails would not eat geraniums. So, in 1996, I planted nothing but the geraniums – pink and crimson, some with variegated or scented leaves – that I had carefully nurtured from the previous September's cuttings. Over the summer, I kept noticing ever-diminishing plants with no petals, but I explained it away as wind or rain damage, or lack of drainage – anything to avoid confronting the alarming evidence that these snails would devour anything in their path. To this day, no one believes me, but I swear it is true. The snails in my garden seemed to be uber-aggressive: nobody else had molluscs that massacred *geraniums*, for heaven's sake.

Power corrupts, and absolute power corrupts absolutely. Like true despots, my snails, having had the run of the garden for so many years, did not take kindly to a new regime – that of a rival despot, who prowled about every evening, chucking them over the hedge. So, in the British spirit of fair play, I planted a little extra of whatever it was that I was trying to grow. Innocently, I expected the animals to reciprocate my thoughtfulness and leave my seedlings unblemished – except for a few politely nibbled leaves at the end of each row. But they refused to play fair, chomping through everything: beans, flowers, the lot. Nothing escaped their ruthless jaws. The only colour in the garden came from the labels, which mocked me with their vivid illustrations of how my bedraggled specimens should look. Stronger measures were required.

In the Nineties, the standard advice regarding garden pests – 'Ex-ter-mi-nate!' – was being replaced by a more benign, holistic approach. The organic movement was going mainstream. New pest-control products included white crystals made of aluminium sulphate or ferrous sulphate, which were sprinkled on the soil round the plants. They were supposed to deter snails without harming other wildlife. Guiltily, I applied the pesticide to my vegetables. But the snails were not deterred. I swear that they snacked on the stuff before moving on to their main course: my beans.

I was at breaking point. It was time to get heavy.

SEVEN

Pellets of Shame

he bright blue pellets were as innocent-looking as sweets.

'Metaldehyde won't hurt them,' a gardening friend said, airily. 'They'll just get a hangover, and they'll feel too sick to eat your plants.'

I trawled back through the hazy memories of my youth. The few hangovers I could remember came in various degrees of awfulness. At worst, I had woken up thirsty, groggy and fuzzy-headed, with a strong aversion to bright sunlight and loud noises. In which case, my snails would get off lightly. They were deaf as a post and could see only vague outlines; as for brightness, the sun had barely made an appearance in the last fortnight. Anyway, they could always withdraw into their shells – the snail equivalent of diving under the duvet.

The day I bought my first tin of metaldehyde pellets is one I will never forget. For at least half an hour, I hung about nervously, picking up the container then putting it back again as I read the warnings: 'harmful to pets and wildlife'; 'remove bodies'. I dithered for a long time before I made a decision. I wondered how many hapless cats would wander into the garden and decide to snack on the blue granules. On the other hand, our two cats, Sparkle and Shadow, turned up their noses at anything except the most expensive cat food, although Sparkle had a penchant for fresh melon. The three cats next door were old, and kept to their own side of the fence – Sparkle and Shadow fiercely guarded their own territory, soon seeing off any neighbouring feline that dared to show its face. So there would be no pet slaughter, the idea was ridiculous. Hedgehogs, field mice and birds never entered my consciousness.

In my heart of hearts, I knew that the pellets were poison. But it was only much later, when reading up on their deadly ingredient, that the full magnitude of my actions hit me. Metaldehyde kills molluscs if they touch, inhale or eat it. It does so by sending their mucus production haywire. In the past, I had often noticed when moving snails that if I brushed their undersides, their first response was to excrete large amounts of slime, which bubbled forth from beneath their bodies to create a halo of froth. This is a response to stress.

A metaldehyde-poisoned snail (or slug) secretes huge quantities of mucus – up to fifty per cent of its body weight. It is trying to increase the activity of the digestive enzymes in its gut, in order to transform the poison into a less toxic substance. But the poison has compromised the effectiveness of these enzymes, and the snail stops feeding as its digestive system breaks down.

It makes a heroic, last-ditch attempt to detoxify its body by producing more mucus, trying to excrete the noxious substance through its slime. But slime production calls for enormous amounts of energy – a resource that the creature no longer has. Without the precious mucus that keeps it lubricated and mobile, it begins to dry up. Meanwhile, the nervous system becomes paralysed. This further prevents movement. Unable to escape to shelter, its plight exacerbated by sunny, dry, or windy conditions, the snail's dehydration process speeds up even faster.

The animal goes into hyperdrive as it tries desperately to rid itself of the poison – by now it is fighting for its life. But this is a losing battle. After its final burst of metabolic activity, it becomes exhausted and grinds to a halt. The cells cease to function and the creature dies.

It is easy, with hindsight, to take a moral stance. But that day in the shop when I bought the odious pellets, I had reached rock bottom. As I walked home, I reckoned that if I sprinkled them very, very sparingly on the earth, I would do the snails little harm. When I got home, I cautiously opened the container. The pellets were round and vivid blue; they looked a bit like Smarties – tempting for small children. But in my garden, there were no babies or toddlers. Later, in the cool dampness of late evening, when I knew the snails would be preparing for their nightly banquet, I scattered a few granules round my vegetables.

I was unprepared for the scene that met my eyes the next morning. I had expected to see one or two bodies lying about the place. But the pellets seemed to have attracted the entire mollusc population of the garden. It was a gruesome sight. The bodies were curled up, stiff and covered in a frothy green slime. Some were twisted into terrible contortions, as if their last moments had been spent in agony. Some were still dying, froth coming out of every aperture. I was shocked and sickened. What on earth had I done?

'You'll get used to it,' a friend said, cheerfully, when I confessed. 'I felt just as you did at first. But think of it this way – it's them, or the plants.'

I had often seen this friend's garden, full of thriving, unnibbled flowers and vegetables. I decided to put a time limit on my experiment. At the end of four weeks, I would appraise the situation. There were two potential outcomes. I might become inured to the snails' suffering and be rewarded by a garden that was full of vibrant colour. Or I would be so disgusted with myself that I would forswear the pellets for ever.

During those weeks, I hated having to pick up the slimy green bodies. How was I supposed to dispose of them? Composting or burning was out of the question, so the only place they could go was the waste bin I kept in the carport. It would be a week until the next rubbish collection, and every time I passed the bin, I felt them reproaching me. In my imagination, they swelled and grew monstrous inside their newspaper shrouds.

I stuck it out for three weeks. Then, one day, I found a shrivelled worm lying on the soil. Its head had been bitten off. Horrified, I wondered which bird had tried it for breakfast, decided that it tasted revolting, then possibly died from the small mouthful it had digested.

I abandoned the experiment. It wasn't worth feeling so rotten for the sake of a few lettuces. And I began to worry, not just about my snails, but about the wider implications of scattering the blue pellets on the soil.

The World Health Organisation classifies metaldehyde as a class II (moderately hazardous) pesticide. It warns of all the effects it can have on mammals, being highly toxic by inhalation, moderately toxic by ingestion, and slightly toxic by dermal absorption. It can irritate skin and eyes. Humans can suffer, too. Inhalation can cause severe irritation of the mucous membranes that line the mouth, throat, sinuses and lungs. Swallowing it causes irritation to the stomach and intestines and can cause kidney and liver damage.

We're unlikely to swallow buckets of the stuff; if we were rash enough to ingest 400mg per kilogram of our body weight, we would collapse and die. But before this happened, we'd suffer the inexorable progress of the symptoms: increased heart rate, panting, asthma, depression of the nervous system, drowsiness, high blood pressure, inability to control the passing of urine and faeces, uncoordination, muscle tremors, sweating, excessive salivation, cyanosis (bluish discoloration of the skin due to lack of oxygen), stupor and unconsciousness.

Metaldehyde has been found in our drinking waters, and this is related to farming practices. The levels are safe, according to European guidelines. Yet a possible link with cancer has not been ruled out. As gardeners, when we sprinkle the little blue pellets round our runner beans, we cannot be sure that our beans will be safe to eat – even though the metaldehyde content of each pellet has been reduced in recent years. The cumulative effect of eating pesticide-ingested produce (on however infinitesimal a scale) week after week, year after year, has not been tested on humans – we are all, in effect, the subjects of a long-term experiment.

In autumn, leaves cascade down from the trees in and around my garden. Sometimes I rake them up straight away and bag them for leaf mould. More often, enjoying the rich, sweet smell of humus, I leave them where they fall to rot down. During my vicious metaldehyde period, I cleared a space in the last autumn's decaying leaves to sow some wild-flower seeds. In the moist soil beneath, trundling about like miniature locomotives, were many centipedes and millipedes. Watching these tiny creatures from my human-world perspective, I wondered what else might be happening in their parallel world. It seems strange, looking back, that while in previous years I had spent so much time reading up on soil structure, I had completely ignored something just as important – the bustling mass of different creatures dwelling in the earth that we dig and weed and plant. In a woeful case of locking the door after the horse had bolted, I began to learn about soil fauna.

Beneath our feet is a network of creatures working together to keep the soil healthy. These microorganisms, worms and insects decompose organic matter, replenish soil nutrients from humus, promote root growth and increase nutrient uptake. They also break down herbicides and pesticides. Some, such as the earthworm, which eats the soil, depositing the earth that moves through its body as nutritious castings, are duly lauded as the gardener's friend. But others are not so kindly welcomed. Snails, like worms, provide nutrient-rich excrement. They might have spent their lives munching through our prize vegetables, but at least they are gracious enough to give them back in the form of organic fertiliser (considering that they eat several times their body weight in food every day, that is an awful lot of carbon, nitrogen and protein packed neatly into one tiny sausage). When alive, they are a good food source for small mammals, reptiles, amphibians and birds. And when they finally die and decompose – by natural means – their bodies and shells nourish the soil with carbon, proteins and calcium. Snails, when we really think about it, are very useful creatures.

Contemplating the billions of creatures beneath my feet as I weeded and planted and watered filled me with awe. It also made me think much harder about the implications of using pesticides, particularly metaldehyde. There was one particular point of information that I could not understand. The pesticide companies assure us that metaldehyde is broken down into harmless substances by soil microorganisms. But, considering all the vital jobs that these tiny creatures are already doing, why give them yet another task?

I began to see the ecosystem within the soil as resembling the human body, with its interconnected and interdependent systems. While the body can cope with a great many of the stresses we lay upon it – alcohol, caffeine, tobacco – there comes a point when the immune system cries out: 'No more!' Then we get ill, often very ill. I dreaded to think of the poisons we were loading into the earth, which nourishes us, and how far we could push before its immune system gave up.

Enough was enough. I vowed that no more snails would die on my watch, except, as a final resort, by organic and painless means. In the future, prevention, rather than control, would be my aim.

EIGHT

Beer Traps

One sunny afternoon, I left my sharpest knife on a plate in the garden, where I had been chopping vegetables, and went indoors to make a cup of tea. When I came back a little later, I found a snail sliming over the upturned blade as it tried to get to a cabbage leaf. The intrepid traveller was perched astride this deadly weapon as if that was the most normal thing to do. How was it that the animal hadn't sliced itself in half, when its body was far softer than the cabbage? I picked it up by the shell and peered at the underside of its foot, expecting to see colourless blood seeping from a huge gash. There was not even a scratch. The snail seemed to have skin tougher than an elephant's hide.

The secret of the snail's amazing ability to traverse the sharpest razor blade without harming its body lies in its slime. This mucus is produced by a gland – the pedal gland – at the front of the creature's foot.

Snails and slugs belong to a class of molluscs called gastropods, whose name comes from the Greek word *gaster*, meaning 'belly', and *podos*, 'footed'. A gastropod slides along on its foot over its own slippery stream of pedal mucus, which acts as a cushion. The snail that was sauntering over the blade of my knife as if merely enjoying an afternoon stroll over my lettuces had resourcefully produced exactly the right quantity and quality of slime to perform this feat with ease.

The mucus enables the snail to creep over a huge variety of surfaces. Soil, gravel, glass – the snail takes them all, literally, in its stride. In the sole of its foot are two sets of muscle fibres that contract and expand as the animal glides along its liquid ribbon. One set of fibres contracts, pulling the snail's tail towards its head, then the second set propels the sole of the foot forward in a ripple-like motion. The tummy-creeping movement of a five- or six-month-old baby trying to reach the rattle that its irritating parent has

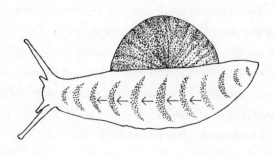

Snail movement.

placed just out of reach is similar to the wave-like progress of the snail's body.

A mollusc has a remarkable ability to adapt the viscosity – stickiness – of its mucus to the terrain it has to negotiate. It does this by altering the amount of pressure it applies to a surface. When it releases the pressure by relaxing its muscles, the mucus becomes more sticky, enabling the snail to attach itself to any object, in any position. Using this clever means, the animal can remain stuck to a vertical wall face, or upside down inside the rim of a flowerpot – usually the one housing somebody's favourite patio plant. By contrast, if the creature decides that it wants to scoot along, the slime becomes thinner as the muscles tense up and apply more pressure. Mucus production is hard work; the snail spends about a third of its energy output on this vital task, far more than it requires for locomotion.

For those who think a snail's slime is somewhat revolting, research has shown that it has some unexpected uses. In South Korea, a skin cream containing snail mucus has become so popular that the shelves cannot be restocked quickly enough to meet demand. It is expensive, of course. Which makes me wonder whether it might not be simpler, and cheaper, to cut out the middleman. This would be a fascinating project for serious research. We just need a few hundred volunteers to take part – people of a curious and pioneering nature who, for an agreed length of time, would be willing to coat their skin with mucus directly from the snail.

I am ashamed to admit that, even after my road-to-Damascus moment with the metaldehyde pellets, I did not immediately morph into a mollusc-loving saviour. The snails had not stopped ravaging my runner beans. They just carried on, in their own sweet way, staging their nightly foraging expeditions. This led to some serious lapses.

I had already written off the biological option: nematodes. These microscopic, worm-like organisms are a non-toxic weapon against various creatures that prey on our plants. They enter the pest's body and release bacteria that prevent the creature from feeding, quickly killing it. Then, when their prey has died, they reproduce inside their host. Research scientists have isolated particular nematodes that kill specific garden pests, such as the codling moth or vine weevil.

In the past, I had used slug nematodes. These work by reproducing inside the slug and causing it to swell up to the point where it may explode. The picture on the packet should have been enough to put me off – it showed a distorted creature with a grotesque swelling on its back. I'm glad to report that I was so horrified by this image that I soon gave up zapping slugs in this particularly gruesome fashion.

At this point, I must declare my position on slugs. I have never bonded with them. Malacologists – mollusc experts – may find them fascinating, even appealing. But to me, they have no redeeming features, no charm at all. The worst thing is their slime, far stickier than snail mucus; it clings horribly to the skin and cannot be washed off. Devious and sly and expert at hiding, they burrow under soil and grit. They curl themselves inside my lettuces to be discovered later in the salad bowl.

Snails, by contrast, seem more open and upfront in their behaviour. They disappear into their shells wherever they happen to be, like small children crouching down and covering their eyes in the belief that they are now invisible. Luckily, the nematodes did not work on snails. My intransigent gastropods were spared, and lived to fight another day. Unexpectedly, I was glad. Not only was my conscience partially salved, but deep down, I did not want my snails to die.

The next lapse was salt. This, if sprinkled round plants, is meant to deter molluscs. If they dive into it, their mucus dries out, and they will shrivel up. Nasty. I was hoping that my snails would be sensible, take one look, and give the substance a wide berth. Instead, the salt seemed to intrigue them. As soon as they poked their heads into it, the salt interacted with their slime and they died a horrible death. As if by a bolt of justice from the universe, my plants also withered and keeled over, due to the extra salinity of the soil. It should have been blindingly obvious to anyone with half an ounce of common sense, but so fixated was I on saving my plants, that by now all rational thought had deserted me.

While gardening organically had become a priority, I was still feeling ambivalent about the snails. I just couldn't decide how to treat them. My morals wobbled widely from day to day. On a good day, I'd decide to leave them alone because I had no right to kill any creature; this, at least, made me feel happier with myself. On bad days, I was still full of righteous indignation. What about my plants? Didn't they, too, deserve to live? For years, I had been trying to grow delphiniums and lupins, my favourite summer flowers. How I longed to see them grow to their full height and grace in the herbaceous border, their delicate pinks and purples forming a pinnacle of beauty. For years, I had waged this summer battle. And every year, I had lost. In the end, the pendulum swung in favour of the plants. The more insubordinate the snails, the more determined – the more obsessional – I became.

I had thrown myself into organics with the zeal of a new convert. In the late Nineties, I enrolled on an organic gardening course, leading to a National Vocational Qualification. I learnt a lot of useful gardening tips, such as how to take cuttings and identify new plants, but mollusc management was not a priority. Our teacher blithely stamped on any snail that crossed his path. (Years later, I can still hear the crunch.) Other organic methods recommended were equally gruesome. Plunging my snails into boiling water was a step too far, and cutting slugs in half was definitely out.

Many of my friends were into permaculture, a holistic and sustainable way of living by recycling resources and cultivating the land without harming any creature. I found it inspiring. I discovered that it was much more than a gardening technique, rather a way of understanding how natural systems work successfully. We can use this knowledge to create self-sustaining systems in all areas of our life. Such applications might be as small and specific as the design of our own gardens, or involve grander schemes, such as planning communities, farms, recreational spaces – even towns and cities.

Permaculture is based on three ethical beliefs: care for the Earth, care for people and the need to distribute resources, such as shelter, food and water, fairly throughout the globe. In order to translate beliefs into practice, a set of guidelines or principles can be applied in many areas, such as the design of our own gardens. The key to success lies in harnessing, storing, and using energy in the most sustainable way so as to live lightly on the planet. Whether we use the natural structure of the soil to grow fresh, nutritious plants, or train our children to turn off lights as they leave a room (an endeavour that would try the patience of a saint), we are contributing to a more resilient household or community.

Reading about permaculture prompted me to make simple changes to my own living space. I installed two barrels to capture and store Devon's plentiful rain; I planted vegetables and flowers together to encourage a diversity of insects in one small plot, trying not to disturb the soil by overdigging. A few years later, making use of my south-facing roof, I installed photovoltaic panels, soon generating most of my own electricity.

I began to realise how my own lifestyle reflected my core beliefs and values. Whether to buy all my food from a supermarket or independent traders; whether to travel by bus, train or car – these were all choices that had to be made on an almost daily basis. I still had far to go in my journey towards sustainability – I would have loved to warm my greenhouse with the body heat of chickens and drain my bath water via waste pipes into an outside water tank – but I fell short of my ideals through lack of practicality and even, dare I say it, laziness. Even so, I was going in the right direction.

Permaculture did not, unfortunately, provide the magic answer to the slug and snail problem, other than feeding the creatures to chickens and ducks.

For a while, I also flirted with the biodynamic movement, hoping that it would solve the snail problem. This holistic approach to cultivation is based on the natural rhythms of the Earth. Gardening is directed by the phases of the Moon – a brilliant idea, backed up by sound theory related to the ebb and flow of water within the leaves and roots of plants. Alas, the practice of it was beyond me, simply because I am constitutionally unsuited to anything that requires routine and regularity. I was too scatty to keep consulting the charts that would tell me at which phase of the Moon I should be planting various crops, let alone keep proper records. Nevertheless, this mysterious method of gardening made perfect sense – to me.

On the subject of snails, the biodynamic method of mollusc control seemed oddly out of kilter with the rest of the philosophy. The advice, at that time, was to kill slugs and snails by plunging them into boiling water and then to dry their bodies in the sun. The next step was to cook them to a crisp in the oven (preferably not with the Sunday dinner) and grind them up into a fine powder. This would be solemnly scattered over the soil to deter their relatives from any further plundering. Needless to say, I never tried this out for myself.

Even so, over several years I enjoyed many meditative and ceremonious activities, such as the biodynamic preparation of cow-horn extract, which has to be diluted several times and stirred vigorously in a barrel until a vortex appears. This is then sprinkled over the earth to encourage fertility. I can vouch for the fact that it did enrich the earth in my garden – more of my seeds germinated, and the seedlings looked healthier. But then, so did my snails, growing fat on the produce. The snail population began to increase.

Barriers, such as coffee grounds, were the next weapon in my armoury. I bought a percolator and started drinking coffee again. As I hadn't touched the stuff since my student days, it had an alarming effect on my heart rate. Undaunted, I saved all the coffee grounds and spread them round my plants. The scent was supposed to deter the pests. Dream on. They loved the scent of the coffee. Whole armies of snails gathered round for long sniffing sessions. Then, emboldened and no doubt drugged to their tentacles, they charged en masse at the nearest juicy young shoots, which happened to be my sunflowers. For years I had aspired to grow the tallest sunflower in my road, but I always ended up with a pathetic row of dead seedlings.

Next, I carefully extracted all the hair from my hairbrush and pestered my hairdresser for sweepings to spread round the plants. As my cat Shadow stalked slow-worms in the garden, I stalked her with a stiff cat brush, much to her amazement, as for years I had cheerfully left her to do her own grooming. The hair intrigued the snails. They approached it gingerly, prodding it gently with their tentacles. Word must have got round, because often I could see whole families gathered there. They seemed to be having some kind of confab. Then one or two of them would cautiously begin to climb over the hair, performing amazing feats of gymnastics – tummy arches and foot flattening. Others dug themselves into the soil and then nudged their shells beneath the hair, forming a tunnel that all the family – kids, granny, granddad and Uncle Fred – slid through with ease.

I bought grit and gravel. Friends assured me that these were snail-proof, so I spent a fortune – and did my back in – hauling it out of the car and round to the back garden. The slugs and snails slid over the lumpy terrain as if over a silk sheet. I spent hours crushing eggshells, eating so many eggs that my cholesterol level must have been rocketing off the scale. The snails gleefully slimed over the crushed shells and wove their way through all the tiny, soil-filled gaps as if I had just provided them with a new extreme sport.

My snails were becoming hardier and hardier. All I was doing was precipitating their progress along some preordained Darwinian path towards survival of the fittest. It was as if I could see evolution taking place before my very eyes.

It was time to up the ante. Beer traps were next. I bought crates of the cheapest beer I could find in the supermarkets and poured it into margarine tubs that I set into the earth. Every now and then, I fished out the drowned bodies, deporting them to the compost heap before pouring new liquid into the tubs. It was a job that needed doing often – they soon filled up with dead molluscs, and often I was busy with other things, so the tubs would begin to stink horribly. Once, I naively sent Nathan, then aged eleven, out to do the dirty deed. He was out there a surprisingly long time.

Recently he confessed that he tasted the cheap beer, but it was so revolting he spat it out. To this day, he remains quite aggrieved by my failure to provide a decent drink.

I took to going out in the late evening, snail hunting. I wanted to catch them just before they started sliming up the sides of the tubs, thus easing my ever-guilty conscience. I managed to save many mollusc lives by chucking them over the fence, but I certainly did not save my sanity.

At the same time, I was trying other methods of prevention. I joined the Henry Doubleday Research Association, an organisation that researches and promotes organic gardening, farming and food. I had volunteered to take part in an experiment to test the efficacy of bran as a barrier. The snails were supposed to gobble it voraciously, then swell up and die. Except that mine did not. They nibbled a little of the bran as an hors d'oeuvre, then moved swiftly on to their main course, my lupins. Because this experiment was in the cause of organic gardening, and the results would be published in the association's magazine, I felt duty-bound to keep close tabs on what was happening and to record it in my diary. This necessitated my going out later and later at night, so that I could catch the little buggers in the act.

One night, I was out in the garden until after ten o'clock; the next until past eleven. On the third night, I was prowling round with my torch at midnight, when, through the open kitchen window, I heard the phone ringing. For me, midnight phone calls are always bad news, so with a feeling of sick dread I dashed into the house.

'Hello?' came a friend's anxious voice. 'Ah, Ruth, so you're still alive! We haven't seen you for ages. You were supposed to be meeting us tonight – remember? I rang a couple of days ago to remind you. We thought you must have had an accident.'

'Sorry,' I said lamely. 'I've been out in the garden, um – weeding. Well, actually, I've been snail baiting . . .'

There was an outraged shriek at the other end of the line.

'You mean that all the while your friends thought you were lying senseless in a ditch somewhere, you were actually out murdering snails? You really need to get a life.'

Senseless. Yes, that was certainly me. I was a serious case of obsessive compulsive disorder. If I were indeed to 'get a life', I had to approach the great snail problem in a completely new way.

NINE

The Prodigal Snail

garden snail called Archie holds the world record for the fastest snail, travelling at a speed of 0.005mph. He performed this amazing feat at the World Snail Racing Championships, an annual event held on the cricket field at Congham in Norfolk. Snails race from an inner circle to an outer circle, marked out on damp white cloth. Archie completed the total distance of thirteen inches in two minutes and twenty seconds. If he'd had enough energy to sustain this speed, he would have been able to cover ten feet in just under twenty-two minutes.

In the summer of 2008, I was sitting in my garden, idly thumbing through an old edition of the *Guinness Book of Records*, wondering whether to donate it to a charity shop, together with many other discarded books belonging to my son Nathan, who had now left home. 'Idle' was the key word here. I had reached the statutory retirement age nearly two years earlier. I had not wanted to give up my satisfying and rewarding work – individually tutoring children with special needs and challenging behaviour, many of whom had been excluded from school. I felt bereft. I desperately missed the children and the buzz of watching them blossom and grow in confidence, thanks to the magic of one-to-one support.

In June, there had been a welcome distraction. A daughter had been born to my son Matthew and his wife, Zenia. They lived abroad, so I had the excitement of flying out to cuddle my newest grandchild. My daughter, Sarah, son-in-law, Chris, and my small grandson Robert had come to stay soon afterwards. Their second child was due in October, and their visit was filled with plans and happy anticipation. But once they had gone back to London, there was an eerie, disconcerting silence in the garden. The house, without non-stop snacks and conversations and the clutter of toys, felt lonely and sterile. It was empty-nest syndrome all over again. Although I had become involved in other projects, they didn't keep me busy enough. I was missing my work. I would have to fall back on that time-honoured reason for hanging up my teaching aids – gardening. But this gentle pastime was, once again, turning out to be more of a frustration than a pleasure.

During the ten years leading up to my retirement, I had been so time-limited that any gardening happened in a blunderbuss fashion. My sporadic sorties into the garden were about flailing around for quick fixes: mowing the grass, hacking down the brambles and shoving a few annuals into the earth, most of which got eaten. As I found out when I retired, my marauding molluscs had once again taken control of the garden. The snails were up to their old tricks, but with more energy than ever before.

This would not do. *I* needed to be in charge. I renewed my battle with the snails, turning it into a personal crusade, with a new series of moral lapses. I was gardening organically, but had discovered ways to hit back at my snails without compromising my ideals, such as putting ferrous phosphate crystals round my plants – which was, in effect, snail slaughter. And once again, out came the gravel, grit and eggshells. Coffee grounds were not included, as I had since found out that caffeine kills many soil invertebrates, including insects, earthworms and mites, but now I added wood ash and Vaseline, moats and copper tape to my list of blockades.

The snails – particularly the juveniles – launched themselves joyfully over this new playground equipment. They would shimmy up the Vaseline that I smeared round the plant pots, in a race to reach the top before the slippery substance defeated them, and would gather at the top, waving their tentacles triumphantly at their more timid friends down below. Land snails are not supposed to be able to swim, but mine did. Bubbling their way across the water-filled moats – sections of guttering placed round my French beans – became part of a snailish version of the triathlon. They sniffed scornfully at the wood ash, regarding it as a minor inconvenience, simply manufacturing more slime in their determined efforts to reach my delphiniums. The copper tape, placed along the edge of my vegetable patch, presented more of a challenge. It was intended to interact with their slime, giving them a nasty electric shock. But it became a rite of passage for the juveniles. In a new, dangerous game of chicken, they dared each other to cross over the metal strip, the last one being dubbed a coward for evermore. How they managed it remains a mystery, but I never once found a sizzled snail.

It was against this background of skirmishes, desperate for a break from it all, that I came to be sitting down on that mid-August afternoon reading amazing facts in the *Guinness Book of Records*. The speed of creatures had always fascinated me. The swiftness of migratory birds and cheetahs on the hunt was awe-inspiring when set against the efforts of humans, who think they are so clever when they manage to run at fifteen miles an hour. Proportionate to their size, the velocity of many earth-creeping creatures was also remarkable – including that of Archie, the champion snail, who could have traversed ten feet in twenty-two minutes.

I wondered how long it would take my snails to travel this far, roughly the same as the distance between the bottom fence in my garden and the retaining wall of the large central flower bed. If I took them away from this haven of theirs (where they were at this minute munching through my lupins), and dumped them by the fence, how long would it take them to return? I imagined them sliming wearily back across the intervening lawn, muttering to each other in snaily language about their rough treatment, before going on the attack once more. After their long journey, they'd probably be so ravenous that they would ravage every plant in sight. I reckoned that my snails, being slower than Archie, could take up to an hour, particularly as they would be travelling through grass. Also, being untrained and undisciplined, they would probably mess about, getting sidetracked by a passing centipede, or decide to have a nap on the way.

Weary with snail baiting, weary with myself – and having nothing much to do on that particular afternoon – I collected a number of snails from the big flower bed and set them down against the bottom fence. I went off to make myself a cup of tea, and then, settling down comfortably with tea, book and the radio, I waited to see what the snails would do next. After twenty minutes I wandered over to the fence to check on their progress. There had been no movement at all. They had all curled up inside their shells, disgusted at this unexpected turn of events. Still, I was in no hurry. I was quite enjoying this new experience of just watching the snails, rather than battling with them. It was one of those sleepy, mid-August afternoons when time seems suspended. The garden was having an afternoon nap. Except for the soft drone of bees and the fluttering of cabbage whites' wings, all was quiet and still.

After a while, a few of the snails stretched out their tentacles and started to explore their new terrain. Soon, they were all sliding off in different directions. Only one or two seemed to be heading back to the lupins. My snails seemed to be extra slow, or just very lazy. At this rate, there was no way that they could be back at home base within two or even three hours. By late afternoon I was getting impatient. I had planned to go out that evening. How frustrating. I would never discover their speed. Nor would I even know if they had returned, because how could I distinguish them from the hundreds of others that had made the central flower bed their home? Unless – *unless!* – I could mark them in some way.

With a sudden surge of energy, I dashed upstairs to my bedroom and rooted around until I found what I was looking for – a pot of lurid red nail polish. Bright Red Desire, it was called. It had been lurking at the bottom of a drawer since the mid Seventies. 'Those were the days, my friend, I thought they'd never end . . .', I hummed, as I collected the snails in a bucket and lifted them out one by one. I dabbed a blob of red on each snail's shell before putting it down on the patio. When they were all dry, I returned them to the fence.

Now it would be very plain whether or not they returned to their favourite feeding ground. I had not even counted them, let alone numbered them. I hadn't a clue what I was doing, nor indeed why I was doing it, but for the first time in months, I had enjoyed being in the garden without obsessing about decimated plants and guzzling gastropods. There was an unusual lightness in my step as I went indoors to make my evening meal. The whole afternoon had been fun, and I had almost forgotten what fun felt like.

The next day, I was too busy to check on the snails' progress, but the day after that, I found at least half of them back in the main flower bed, eagerly demolishing a new delphinium I had rashly bought the previous weekend. I gathered up all the red-blobbed snails I could find, marched them down to the bottom of the garden and popped them over the fence. (I wouldn't want my neighbours to think I make a habit of this.) I was curious to know whether these pig-headed snails would climb tenaciously back over the fence or instead go off to find lunch elsewhere. For a few days, nothing happened. But a week later, most of them were back again. Plainly, the menu on offer in the new garden was not to their taste.

By now, I was intrigued. I wondered how far I could take the snails before they admitted defeat and didn't come back. About forty yards from my back garden is a small plot of wasteland. Long grass and nettles, shrubs and small trees grow here; in late May, I sometimes gather fragrant flower heads of elder blossom to make into cordial. If my snails were to make their way home this time, they would have to cross two fences or return through some cycle gates, crawl along the road for a bit until they came to my front hedge, then make their way through my front garden and round the side of the house until they were back on home ground. I gathered up all the red-spotted snails I could find and put them in a bucket. Then, creeping out in the dead of night to avoid the curious eyes of playing children, I dumped them in the long grass.

I never saw them again. I assumed that they were just exhausted from their recent reluctant journeys, or perhaps had slimed into my neighbour's garden and were tucking into his patio plants instead of mine. Curiously, I was disappointed. I wanted the snails to come back. I wanted to see how far they would travel to return to their precious flower bed.

TEN

Location, Location, Location

ate summer, 2009: harvest time. Purple Victoria plums and crisp, long runner beans clustered round their poles; succulent tomatoes, orange-red, weighed down their vines. The garden had generously offered up its fullness, and now seemed to be resting from its labours.

The snails, however, were active, foraging purposefully among all this abundance. They were becoming a real problem for me – but in a new, unexpectedly positive way. It was not so much that these persistent pests were, as ever, demolishing my precious harvest, but that my priorities had changed. A spirit of scientific enquiry had seized me, overriding the need to preserve my plants. I wanted to find out the homing distance of my snails – a quest that had taken on a life of its own. And once I get a bee in my bonnet about something, it is hard to shake it away.

That summer, I'd continued with my unscientific experiments, marking the snails' shells and taking them further and further away from my garden. I'd finally reached the point where I couldn't bear to kill them. Barriers were certainly not working, so the only solution was to move them to new ground. The question was, would they settle in a different environment, and if so, where? Supposing this new location was not to their liking, would they come back again, ravenous as ever? Was there an optimum distance, at which point they would simply throw up their tentacles and admit defeat? So many questions.

I had to start somewhere, so I began to do some tentative research on snail habitats. From the library, I borrowed the book that became my bible: *A Field Guide to the Land Snails of Britain and North-West Europe*, by M. P. Kerney and R. A. D. Cameron. I loved the colour illustrations showing the great variety of species in their many shapes and sizes. Diagrams showed their surprisingly complex internal organs, contrasting with the simplicity and beauty of their shells. When at last I had to return the book to the library, a friend lent me his precious copy. Eventually, I bought my own.

All snail species have a habitat to which their anatomy and physiology is adapted. Lime-loving molluscs thrive on the alkaline wetlands of fens and the edges of rivers. Grassland, rocks and cliffs all have their own inhabitants. But these locations would be entirely unsuitable for garden snails. Over the centuries, this species has naturalised in our gardens. Ever since we began to cultivate our plots with juicy vegetables and attractive flowers, *Cornu aspersum* has been muscling its way in, creating mayhem for gardeners. Yet I wanted to be kind to these creatures. If they were to be forcibly repatriated, the least I could do was to find them somewhere they could settle.

Of all the possible habitats, woodlands are the richest. Damp and cool, they offer a place to shelter and a diet of woodland plants. Once, most of Europe was covered with forests. Today, a woodland with lime-rich soil that has not been disturbed by logging might host forty species of snail. My nearest woodland, on the edge of a park with play equipment and football posts, was about a quarter of a mile away. It sloped down towards a stream. Because the track leading down there was uneven and muddy, it was largely undisturbed, except by the occasional dog walker and exploring children. Alders, beeches, birches and sycamores formed a cool green canopy overhead, while the ground was covered by grass, ivy and nettles. In spring, primroses, celandine and bluebells, buttercups and dandelions bloomed; as the seasons changed, different wild flowers sprang up. My snails would just have to change their diet a little and learn not to be so fussy.

I imagined they would feel at home there. Snails feel happiest where their new habitat most resembles the original location. If they were pining with homesickness, there were plenty of safe mollusc service stations – roadside verges, parks, hedges, ditches and other gardens – along the return route.

Even so, it was a long and dangerous trek. They would first of all have to find their way out of the woodland, heading in the right direction towards the park. This huge

open area was always filled with children kicking footballs
and dogs chasing sticks. Even if the snails weren't crushed
underfoot, their nail-polish blobs would make them an easy
target for circling birds or prowling small mammals looking
for a tasty snack. If they did somehow manage to crawl,
unscathed, to the other side of the green, they would then
have to negotiate the traffic on two minor roads and cross a
car park before finally reaching the small wasteland area at
the end of our cul-de-sac. It was impossible, surely? They
could never do it, not in a hundred years. And yet . . .

In the past, from different local sources, I had heard
amazing stories of snail homing. One lady told me she had
taken her snails down to the river Dart, a mile and a half
away, and that they had all, in dribs and drabs, come back
the following year. Other apocryphal stories involved
amazing feats of endurance and stamina. I heard about snails
that scaled church towers or twenty-foot walls, crossed fast-
flowing rivers and busy roads, all for the sake of their
much-loved vegetables.

I searched everywhere for information on snail homing.
I found plenty of articles about the extraordinary journeys
of other creatures, great and small, and these were fascinating in themselves. The bar-tailed godwit spends its
summer in New Zealand, but goes to South Alaska to breed.
Once there, one might expect it to rest on its laurels, but no:
it turns round and flies, at twenty miles an hour, back to
New Zealand. This gruelling flight takes only seven or eight
days, even in extreme conditions, such as wind and storm.
The Arctic tern flies nearly twenty thousand miles from the
South to the North Pole; the grey whale swims back and

forth up the west side of North America. Every year, salmon battle many miles upstream to spawn, somehow remembering how to reach exactly the same stretch of river where they hatched. Even tiny, fragile creatures can have this amazing homing ability and incredible powers of endurance. The monarch butterfly migrates from Canada to Mexico in autumn, laying its eggs and then returning home. Leatherback turtles, homing pigeons, mole rats – all have this remarkable instinct.

Could my meandering molluscs steer a straight, determined line back to my dahlias? Other creatures that homed had good reasons for doing so: they needed to breed or find food – or both. When the humble limpet leaves its home, floating away on the tide to feed, it always returns to exactly the same niche in a rock. Could *Cornu aspersum* match the ability of its not-too-distant relative? Having become so attached to my tasty home-grown plants, might it decide that it was well worth expending a great deal of slime for the sake of such paradise? There was only one way to find out.

One evening in September, after dark, I crept across the park. There was no one about except a small group of teenagers, sitting on a large fallen log that doubled as a seat. They were behaving themselves impeccably, quietly chatting. As I passed by, they all fell silent, watching me. It was plain that they thought I was Up To No Good. The clues might have been the large green bucket and the torch I was carrying. As I disappeared into the woodland's dark entrance, I could feel their eyes boring into me. I was worried that they would all follow me, so I hurried on and hid in the nearest clump of trees. All was quiet, so I switched on my torch and crashed about in the nettles and brambles until I found a suitable place to release my snails. I reckoned that the little creatures would be well provided for among the clumps of arum, yellow archangel and wood anemone.

Suddenly, I realised that I had not painted their shells. Somehow, I had managed to forget this vital stage of the experiment. I would have no means of telling whether or not the snails had returned. Feeling stupid and frustrated, I hurried back out of the woodland, again running the gauntlet of the teenagers, who fell silent. They looked at me and then at the bucket as if it held a dismembered corpse.

The exercise had not been a total waste of time. I'd found a possible new land for the emigrating molluscs, and during the next two weeks I managed to transport quite a few of my troublemakers to their sylvan retreat, remembering, in the end, to mark them. But if they were intending to come back, they'd have to start out on their journey very soon – it was now autumn, when snails shrink into their shells in preparation for the cold winter ahead, sealing themselves up in their protective membrane. I doubted whether they would bother to return this year.

I did not begrudge the time I had spent taking my snails to the woodland – it had been fun, and I had saved a few plants in the process. But I realised that I had left it too late to discover their homing distance. I would have to put my experiments on hold.

In the garden of each of my homes, there has always been a special tree. When I was a child, the old apple tree provided a comforting hiding place, a piece of gymnastic equipment and the challenge of reaching for the highest apples. In Surrey, the gnarled wisteria linked me to gardens past – and to my foolish, forsaken dreams of affluent living. My favourite tree of all is the mature silver birch that resides in my Devon garden. It stands in the right-hand bottom corner, graceful and willowy, so tall that it seems to touch the clouds.

It was not always so. When Nathan and I moved in, the tree was a thin, stunted, fragile specimen, choked almost to death by a row of leylandii. We took these down and, as if in gratitude, the silver birch took a huge breath and soared upwards, tall and free. From my window, I can gauge the strength of the wind by the dance of its slender branches. Should a faint breeze ruffle their pendulous skirts, they sway in gentle stirrings, a slow-dance embrace. When a gale blows, every branch, leaf and twig whirls and swirls in a fiery, passionate flamenco.

The silver birch has been called the Lady of the Woods. Legend associates it with healing, and with new starts and beginnings. Someone once told me that it is also known as the Listening Tree. Strange though it may sound, I have shared with my tree both my happiest moments and my worries, placing my hand on the papery white bark and looking up into its branches. Sometimes it grows very still, with a special attentiveness; sometimes it sways, extra vigorously, as if in sympathy.

So it came about that I was at the bottom of my garden, in late 2009, with my arm round the trunk of my faithful

Listening Tree, sighing out all my troubles, large and small. Included in the mix was the problem of my snails. My haphazard foray into the scientific world had stressed me out. I asked the tree to help me find a way forward with my homing research.

November closed in, bringing dark evenings and cold, damp days. The garden, with its drooping, frostbitten leaves, folded in on itself. It was that quiet, winding-down time before Christmas, a period for reflection and for replenishing my inner forces, in harmony with the resting garden outside my window. I could feel my own energy drawing down, to the point where the simplest task became an effort. When at home, all I wanted to do was to sit and read, or listen to the radio. At times, I felt extra tired, and worried that I was heading for some dread illness. Or maybe I was just getting old.

The radio provided distraction and company. Without fail, I would listen to my favourite Radio 4 programme, *Material World*, in which four or five new scientific discoveries or phenomena were explained each week by experts. During the past couple of years, I had become addicted to the programme. For one thing, I understood most of the science. The presenter had the knack of eliciting key pieces of information from the physicists, chemists, geologists and astronomers who were so expert in their own fields, then distilling the salient points to make this new knowledge accessible to untutored minds, such as mine.

January brought treacherous, icy conditions on roads and pavements. One particular Thursday, coming home wearing highly unsuitable wellies, I skidded twice, landing on my coccyx. I hobbled into the house, having missed most of *Material World*. Gasping for a cup of tea, I put the kettle on and switched on the radio. The word 'award' caught my attention. *Material World* was inviting listeners to submit ideas for research in a project called 'So You Want to be a Scientist?'. Out of all the entries, four finalists would be selected. They would all be given expert help by a mentor, and the winner would be named Amateur Scientist of the Year.

I had entered only two prize-winning contests in my life. As a child, my art entry had gone astray in the post; the second, inventing a catchphrase in a holiday magazine, resulted only in a mountain of junk mail. Would I strike it lucky this time?

For several weeks, I carried the thought round in my head, mulling it over, but doing nothing about it. For one thing, I reckoned that other people would have far more brilliant ideas with much wider appeal. Who, apart from me, was interested in snails? For another – and this sounds really stupid – I was not sure that I could manage all the online stuff. I avoided doing anything on my computer unless truly necessary, and then I would approach the infernal machine gingerly, with trepidation, as if it might blow up in my face. This technophobia went back a long way, together with complete incompetence. Even submitting my idea online would be a challenge. It just went to prove that I could never be a scientist, not even an amateur one. Real scientists navigated the electronic world with ease and enthusiasm, producing graphs and tables and maps. And they loved doing it. To them, it was as easy as making a cup of tea.

Yet some inner wisdom told me that if I missed this opportunity, I would regret it. Just before the deadline, at the end of February, I typed a one-hundred-word explanation of my research idea into the required option box on the computer – this in itself felt like a major achievement – and sent it off to the *Material World* team. My question: how far away do I have to dump my snails before they lose the ability to find their way back to my garden?

ELEVEN

Data Sets

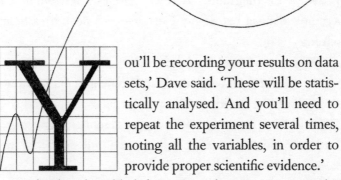

'Y ou'll be recording your results on data sets,' Dave said. 'These will be statistically analysed. And you'll need to repeat the experiment several times, noting all the variables, in order to provide proper scientific evidence.'

I gulped and nodded, hoping to disguise my panic by stuffing down another mouthful of scone. Dave Hodgson was my new science mentor. A population ecologist and statistician based on the University of Exeter's Cornwall Campus, he lectures and researches terrestrial biodiversity in all its glorious forms. He was enthusiastic and cheerful, exuding a reassuring air of complete confidence. He and Michelle Martin, the capable, calm project manager who would be in charge of all four 'So You Want to be a Scientist?' finalists, were sitting round my living-room table sampling a Devon cream tea. I had just collected them from the station, Michelle having travelled down from London carrying some expensive and complicated-looking sound equipment. This was to record my first discussions with a real, live scientist and my lamentations of despair at my plundered plants. They both wanted to see the garden and my snails at work, but their main mission was to initiate me into the alien arena of scientific experiments. I was soon to be dragged, kicking and screaming, into the scary world of numbers.

Transfixed, I watched as Dave covered a sheet of file paper with diagrams. Arrows, circles and unfamiliar symbols danced before my eyes. I took a deep breath and asked:

'What *is* a data set, exactly?'

Michelle and Dave blinked, and somehow managed not to look at one another. They must have suspected that I would have limited knowledge of scientific procedure, but they clearly hadn't predicted the full extent of my inexperience.

Obligingly, Dave drew a table with columns and headings and launched into an explanation. I grabbed another scone and tried to look intelligent. Just before leaving, Michelle said casually, 'I'll set you up with a Facebook page.' This was a hundred times scarier than any data set. I was about to meet my Waterloo – technology.

After submitting my research idea to 'So You Want to be a Scientist?' in February 2010, I had almost forgotten about it. That winter was harsh, and seemed to last for ever. The garden was a grey, dismal mass of drooping, frost-withered stems. Nothing could be further from my mind than snails and all their shenanigans.

Then, in late March, Michelle rang up. Out of thirteen hundred entries, I was on a shortlist of forty. The judges must have taken my idea seriously. Maybe it wasn't quite as silly as I had started to believe. A couple of weeks later, there was another call from the BBC. I had reached the last ten. Michelle wanted to know whether, if selected as one of the four finalists, I was prepared to devote a whole summer to the experiments.

'It will be hard work,' she warned.

'No problem!' I said cheerfully.

Playing with snails for weeks on end: how arduous could that possibly be? Anyway, it was gratifying enough to be in the last ten; I did not expect to get any further. I listened to the *Material World* episodes in which we ten finalists explained our ideas for research. We were a mixed bag. One person wondered if playing music to bees would increase their productivity and the quality of the honey. An artist suggested putting a mannequin, apparently browsing, in his showroom window to see if it would attract more customers. The judges must have had great fun selecting a suitable topic among so many quirky and imaginative ideas, but no doubt it was difficult, too. For a start, the idea – or hypothesis – had to lend itself to a clearly designed experiment that was neither too off-the-wall nor too expensive. It had to be practical. So drilling a hole through the centre of the Earth, or exploding a bomb in the eye of a hurricane, were ideas that would not make the shortlist. The parameters of the research had also to be clearly defined and not bogged down with too many variables. It should possibly have some useful application in the field of science. Above all, the idea should engage *Material World* listeners.

I returned from holiday in mid-April, just in time for another phone call from Michelle. I was in the chosen four. The final would be held in the middle of September, giving me five months to prepare. It dawned on me that this summer would be no mere snail-hunting romp in the garden. The hard work was about to begin.

Before finding the homing *distance* of snails – i.e. how far away from home they can be, yet still find their way back – I had first of all to demonstrate by experiment (rather than anecdote) that they have a homing *instinct*. This is an inborn ability, written into their genetic make-up, that can guide them home to their resting or feeding sites from wherever they have been wandering. With Dave's guidance, I devised an experiment that would reveal whether or not my snails were returning to their home base through instinct. It was important to prove that this was not a random movement towards food or shelter, but that these were home-loving creatures that preferred to settle in one place and would return to it again and again.

To prove instinct, I had to establish a base to which the snails might return. This could be any part of my garden in which the snails liked to congregate. On my data set, this would be recorded as 'Home', and I would collect a number of snails from there. Then, I must find a second patch, which a different group of snails seemed to favour. Snails collected from this site would be my 'Away' sample. The terms 'Home' and 'Away' were interchangeable, being simply a way of distinguishing between the two groups; they could equally have been labelled A and B. Each sample could be collected from either a resting or a feeding site: snails often move between the two, but tend to stay for a while in one or the other. The point was to prove that from whichever favourite haunt I whisked them, they would return, like exiles to their beloved homeland.

All would have their shells marked with some kind of paint, a different colour for each sample. Then, both groups would simultaneously be released from a central testing area, midway between the two bases. I would then monitor the progress of the snails to see how many were canny enough to go back home.

This did not sound too daunting. What was much scarier was the data set on which I had to record my findings. Dave had explained that it was a spreadsheet with columns, and had drawn out a rough sketch as a guideline.

I studied Dave's sketch carefully. It was clear and logical. At the top of my spreadsheet, there would be a main heading to describe the experiment. I would state the date on which it was carried out, the number of snails in each sample, the colour of their markings, the length of the testing distance, and a brief description of the two locations they had been collected from.

Below this were seven columns, each with their own heading: Date of release; Dates of recovery; #Home snails returned to Home base; #Home snails crossed over to

Away base; #Away snails returned to Away base; #Away snails crossed over to Home base; Weather conditions on day of experiment.

Even I could manage that, I thought – although at first I couldn't for the life of me work out what # meant. I just had to be prepared to meet my nemesis, the computer, and enter the information on it.

This was exciting. It felt as though I were returning to something special, engaging at last in something I'd missed out on. Now, I had a chance to make up for the lost years. Best of all, it was the perfect excuse to spend hours in *my* natural habitat – the garden. This was going to be fun. I couldn't wait to get going.

To begin, all I had to do was round up my most recalcitrant troublemakers and keep them in some kind of holding bay while I applied distinctive markings to their shells. Dave had reassured me that this would not harm the snails in any way. I already had several pots of acrylic paint. Easy! Just to be sure, I grabbed a few of the unsuspecting victims that were noshing on my French beans and dolloped a blob of paint on each one. The paint, which adhered so well to paper, simply spread out thinly over the smooth shells, merging with the brown bands before dripping onto each poor creature's foot.

Another method was needed. I remembered the Bright Red Desire that I had used a couple of years ago. I stood by nail-polish counters in shops, trying out as many colours as I could. Very soon, I ran out of fingernails, and my hand was a hotchpotch of flashy colours. I had no way of knowing which of these would best 'take' on the surface of the shells. The silver and gold would surely shine like beacons and attract predators, yet the more subdued colours – maroons, dark blues and greens – were perhaps too subtle. Would they show up on the brown speckles? I could not make up my mind. The trouble was that I rather loved all of them. It felt like having to choose an outfit for a special occasion and longing to take home all the ones that fitted and looked good. But at least I could afford the nail polish, just about, and it was all in the cause of science. In the end, I bought fifteen, attracting some odd looks at the checkout when I held out my polish-daubed hand for the change.

The best place to find snails was on the patio outside my back door, where I could keep an eye on them. I was still struggling with the term 'Home'. I tend to take things literally and, despite Dave's careful explanation that this location – as with the Away base – could be anywhere in the garden, I was still half-wedded to the idea that Home should be near the house. Happily, the best place for my Home base *was* the patio.

I hunted round the garden for the snails that were about to make mollusc history. But, as if by some unanimous accord, they suddenly disappeared. I asked Dave's advice. There was only one solution: in order to establish a Home base, I would have to lay down snail bait. By early May, my bait – petunias and hostas – was in place in pots on the patio.

To help the judges follow my progress, I had started writing an online diary.

6 May: I put out bait to attract the Home snails. I can't believe there are so few of them this spring. I want them to home to the petunias and hostas and French marigolds under their own steam, without my putting them there. But when I looked, all I could find was one tiny snail, sealed up in his/her epiphragm under the sill of the patio doors. Has the cold spell killed them off, or are they just being awkward? It feels really weird to actually want them to eat my plants!

7 May: Still no snails. Went to the market today and bought a BIGGER hosta . . . I want to wait as long as possible to attract the snails naturally to the homing patch, rather than introduce them artificially, so will wait a few more days.

During the next week, I rooted about in all the most likely mollusc hiding places, morning, noon and evening. On 11 May at 6pm, I noted that at last things seemed to be happening. I discovered that a sizeable number of the flowers on the large petunia cluster had been nibbled. On investigation, all I found was one lone slug. I had been tempted to import snails from elsewhere in the garden and force-feed them on the bait plant until they loved it so much that they stayed for ever. But this would be cheating. I needed snails that had a natural home.

I went back to the patio later that evening. Two metres away from the bait, I found some snails idling under the patio sill, and another five among some day-lily leaves in the corner of the garden next to the patio door. I left them where they were, to see what they would do next. At 8.30am and 8.30pm, I checked their progress. I expected, as it was late, to see them sliming determinedly towards the bait, but one snail had gone back to sleep under the sill and the others were in exactly the same position I'd left them in. Raising the question: had they gone into shock?

I realised that the day-lily patch and the patio sill were their resting places, from which they would sneak out to feed on the bait in the dead of night. But it did seem, at last, that I had succeeded in establishing a Home base. For the purposes of this experiment, because the snails were continually moving between the three sites, this area could be considered one base. I was sure that a true scientist would remain on watch by the petunias all night, torch, snack and notebook in hand. I was far too fond of my sleep.

The problem still remained that there were so few snails, only ten so far. Ideally, I would have liked between fifteen and twenty in each group. This was so disappointing: the experiment had not even started; the bait had hardly been nibbled. After years of giving me grief and aggravation, the snails had downed tools and scarpered. They were all in cahoots to scupper my experiment. Some kind of snailish communication system was at work, an early warning system that said, in effect: 'Watch out – she's after you!'

I was reading about how snails' behaviour is related to their physiology when I came up with another reason for their sudden absence. This was just my own hypothesis (by now I was well into the scientific terminology), but it did appear to offer a much more rational explanation than a wilful, all-out strike. My theory was connected with how the snails fitted into the grander scheme of things.

Taxonomy is the science of classifying species into a hierarchy of ranks: kingdom; phylum; class; order; family; genus; species. Garden snails are in the animal kingdom (as opposed to the plant kingdom). They reside in the phylum known as Mollusca, meaning 'soft-bodied ones'. Taxonomists have identified the common features within this phylum as (among others) a shell, a muscular mouth and a soft body. Animals in this group can dwell on land, in freshwater or seawater.

The next category is a class, which takes in all animals that have broad attributes in common. The phylum Mollusca includes the classes Bivalvia (which encompasses oysters) and Cephalopoda (including octopuses). Snails belong to the class Gastropoda, which covers seventy thousand species, including slugs and limpets. Gastropoda means 'stomach foot', referring to the way that creatures within this group creep along on their bellies.

Within this class, garden snails are members of a subgroup called pulmonates, which breathe air through lungs rather than gills. They belong to the order Stylommatophora, 'stalk-eyed ones' – named after the eyes at the tips of their tentacles – and their family is Helicidae, from the Greek *helix*, or 'spiral'. The genus is *Cornu*, meaning 'horn' in Latin – it also means 'strong' and 'hard'; the species *aspersum* – 'scattered' or 'speckled'. A species is the most basic unit of taxonomy. Creatures within this category are able to interbreed and produce fertile offspring.

Knowing how my snails fitted into this tree of life was satisfying. I hoped that it would give me some clues as to my snails' sudden desertion. I liked the descriptive terms, particularly the expression 'stalk-eyed'. To me, those miniature eyes, waving about on the ends of its tentacles, are one of the garden snail's most intriguing features – so versatile, capable of remarkable flexibility. I wondered if the snails' sudden disappearance from my garden was connected with these stalk eyes.

A snail has two pairs of stalks. They are retractable, turning outside-in, like the fingers of a glove, as they disappear into the body. The eyes are on the upper pair, and are very simple organs. They allow the creature, just about, to tell the difference between light and darkness, and to give it a rudimentary idea of shapes and form, as well as a sense of direction. The lower stalks are for smell and taste; the snail uses all of these senses to locate its favourite feeding and resting sites.

Once, I accidentally dropped a doughnut in the garden. It was clearly a goner, so I left it while I went inside to find something else for my teatime snack. I got sidetracked by a long telephone call, and it was much later before I went out again. Converging on the doughnut in a wide arc, like iron filings round a magnet, were dozens of snails. This unexpected bounty had enticed all the patio snails out of their pots and crevices. I could see their lower tentacles waving about, positively drooling, as they slimed towards the food. Intrigued by the snails' attraction to sweet things, I decided to do a mini-experiment on the spot. I brushed off some of the sugar from the doughnut, mixed it with some water in a saucer, and waited to see what would happen. I watched one snail climb into the saucer and then stop short as soon as its sole touched the sugar mixture. 'Mmmm! Even better!' it must have thought, as it sucked up the solution.

Molluscs are also sensitive to touch and to movement, as anyone who has ever prodded a snail's fleshy foot will know. If I touched any part of their skins, they would immediately disappear inside their shells. Although they have no hearing – they do not possess any organ that corresponds to what we know as ears – they do feel vibrations through the ground. These reverberate through the sensitive cells of their feet and warn their primitive brains of danger.

Armed with this knowledge, I could understand, or at least hazard a guess, as to why my snails kept disappearing whenever I tried to track them down. They had not credited me with evil intent – there was possibly a more scientific explanation. My almost constant presence in the garden, my repeated efforts to lure them from their food and resting places, could have left traces of my scent, which they could easily smell. As I repeatedly bent over their hidey-holes and crashed about, my footsteps, my scent and the shadow of my body probably sent them into a state of red alert. No wonder they all upped sticks and sought refuge elsewhere.

As for the telepathy, maybe this was not such a mad idea after all. Snails excrete pheromones – a kind of chemical messenger – in their slime. This helps other snails to follow their trails. Perhaps, once a few stalwarts began the mass exodus, their more timid companions were tempted to tag along, maybe sensing trouble, or hoping that these silvery ribbons of mucus led to new gastronomic delights. This theory sounds more scientifically plausible, but I still prefer the idea that these intriguing creatures communicate purely by thought transference.

TWELVE

Love Darts

For almost a week, I seldom ventured out into the garden. I hoped to lull the snails into a sense of false security, tempting them to relax and to recolonise their old feeding and resting sites.

By 17 May, I needed to get down to business. I was anxious to set up my first instinct experiment, and I needed two large samples of snails. So one morning in mid-May, I rose at the crack of dawn. This was the snails' happy hour. They slimed about in huge numbers, feasting on the dew-drenched vegetables. It was a perfect time to catch them, yet usually I was still fast asleep. Early-bird friends assured me that this was the best time of day, yet to me it presented an eerie, spookily grey, godforsaken no-man's-land. But desperate measures were now called for, and I padded outside in my bare feet.

A damp, earthy sweetness assailed my nostrils. Every petal, every plant seemed to be in competition to produce the most alluring scent; honeydew, lilac, and the faint bouquets of various blossoms all mingled together. Every blade of grass sparkled with dew. A thin sliver of orange sun rose just above the horizon; shafts of gold and pink permeated the soft blanket of mist that wrapped round the hills, glinting on windowpanes and aerials and burnishing the tops of trees and hedgerows. All was silent. Even the birds were still asleep.

Almost drunk with the heady delight of it all, I crept over the paving stones like a stalking cat – I was convinced that the snails could feel my lightest footfall through the vibrations in their skin, and I was determined to give them no advance warning of my presence. My toe nudged up against something soft and squishy. I looked down, and saw an extra-large, lumpy snail. On closer inspection, it was two snails, coupled close together. From each of their bodies protruded something large, round and milky white. The two things – which looked suspiciously like penises – were tightly coiled together like a thick cable. It seemed that I had stumbled across a pair of mating snails.

It was difficult to see an actual opening. Each penis appeared to be coming out of the same hole in each creature's head that its partner's penis was disappearing into. This seemed a very strange way of going about things.

Snails, I had already discovered, are great exhibitionists. When engaged in their courtship ritual, they have no modesty at all, coupling out in the open for all to see. Nor do they have any health and safety issues. The previous year, walking along the coastal path on the Gower Peninsula, I had almost trodden on two *Cornu aspersum* in full flow, right in the centre of the path. It was surprising enough just to see them in such an unusual location, well away from their usual domestic habitat. There was no juicy food around – only coastal plants such as gorse, viper's-bugloss and sea campion. Not their usual fodder. Yet there they were, happily mating, with no fear of being crushed by human feet or becoming a buy-one-get-one-free breakfast for a passing bird. Perhaps two solitary snails, lost and far from home, had met by chance in this lonely place and just fallen into each other's arms, so to speak.

I contemplated the two interlocked snails on my patio. Maybe they, too, had decided that it was a short life but a merry one. Their newest clutch of eggs would mature into hungry babies just in time to catch the first juicy shoots of my spring vegetables. It seemed highly impertinent to intrude on such an intimate moment. I left them to get on with it while I went in search of other, single, snails, making a mental note to find out more about snail reproduction as soon as I could.

'Intimate moment', I discovered later, was a huge under-statement. The courtship ritual and eventual pairing of snails takes many hours. Because they are hermaphrodites, snails have intricate reproductive systems, each possessing male and female organs. All snails have a common sexual entrance: the front door to the whole system. This opening joins the common genital atrium – a pipe-like passageway, which divides into corridors, leading to separate male and female reproductive organs, including the vagina and penis,

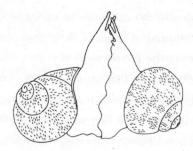

The courtship ritual.

which is normally tucked inside the animal. At the appropriate stage in the mating process, the penis pops out – or everts – through the common sexual entrance by means of blood pressure. After copulation, it is retracted back into the body by a very strong muscle.

It is difficult not to anthropomorphise what appears to be very romantic behaviour, followed by some extraordinary foreplay. First of all, the two snails do a kind of circling dance round each other, frequently caressing with their tentacles. As they move, they secrete a large amount of slime. This forms a platform beneath them, like a silvery skating rink. Then they raise the soles of their feet off the ground, standing almost upright, and clutch one another in an embrace. Wrapping the edges of their soles round one another like cloaks, they rock their bodies, stretching out their tentacles to the fullest extent. After a while, each snail shoots a love dart into the body of its partner.

The dart is a tiny, beautifully sculpted love weapon made of lime. Along its length are ribs that protect and guide it. One end is as sharp as a harpoon, and is designed to pierce flesh. The other end fans out, like the end of an arrow. The dart is not the penis: the exchange of sperm is a totally separate part of the mating process. The purpose of the love dart is to increase the chances of reproduction. Each dart contains a special mucus that causes part of the female half of the reproductive system to temporarily contract, shortening the distance that the sperm must travel before reaching the chamber where the eggs are stored. It is probable that this specialised mucus contains pheromones that help protect and store the sperm within the body of its partner. It's also a means of eliminating rival sperm. During the mating season, a snail might receive sperm from many different partners. This would all be stored, sometimes for months, ready to fertilise the egg at the appropriate time. The successful darter injects a chemical designed to inhibit the efficacy of this product, thus knocking out all its competitors and increasing its own chances of reproduction.

As the snails reach a climax of passion, both simultaneously shoot a dart deep into the other's body like an arrow. Sometimes this foreplay goes sadly wrong; snails need a bit of practice before they become accomplished lovers. Darting can be so forceful that the dart gets buried in the internal organs, causing damage, or even worse, protrudes out of the other side of the recipient's body. Darting can also be woefully inaccurate. Because of its limited sight, the snail cannot see well enough for a good aim. One third of darts fail to penetrate the skin, or miss their target altogether. Happy, though, is the snail that is accurate with its dart, as it will be more likely to reproduce.

In order to trigger successful dart formation, a first mating is necessary – an almost impossible chicken-and-egg situation. Often, the creature mates without yet having 'grown' its first dart. This will reduce its chances of fertility on this particular occasion, but after that, with dart production well established, all should, in theory, be plain sailing. Except that, even after dart formation is up and running, there is another hurdle: after each mating, it takes about week to grow a new dart.

Eventually, after the darting process has finished – often after hours – the snails align themselves so that their common sexual openings are next to each other. Then, each snail inserts its penis into its partner. Across species, the size of the penis varies enormously. Even between different species with the same body size, there are large variations in the size of this organ. One theory is the 'lock-and-key' principle, nature's way of ensuring that mating occurs only between snails of the same species.

Sperm is exchanged in a long, thin package called a spermatophore, a string-like structure similar to toad spawn, which holds the sperm together. This travels through a winding, tunnel-like duct, where it is broken down and the sperm stored in the spermatheca, a tiny balloon-shaped bag. (Sperm can be stored for months: snails instinctively know when the weather conditions are right for fertilisation. Then, they swim towards the female reproductive organs, where they fertilise the eggs.) Meanwhile, the snails, exhausted by their long and energetic mating process, curl up in their shells and rest. Their post-coital slumber can last for hours, even days.

The sun was rising, and so was the temperature. I needed to get my experiment under way before my subjects sank into a heat-induced torpor and refused to cooperate. My two patio lovers were still locked together in their marathon clinch. Unwilling to part them, I continued with my snail hunt. First of all, I had to find a good number in the Home base. Next, I needed to choose an Away base, from which another group of snails could be found. Then I needed to measure the testing distance and designate a central testing area. This was a challenge in itself, and perhaps the trickiest part of the experiment, because I had to find a location exactly midway between the two collection points. Here, I would place a large, shiny, tin tray that would provide a smooth passage for the snails. On it, I had already drawn a circle, divided into segments like a pie chart, with eight compass points marked on it: N, NE, E, SE, etc. The central testing area had to be a neutral space, a patch of grass or paving without food, which would be unattractive to snails. The problem was that the garden was blocked with obstacles of all kinds – stonework and flower beds. I would be hard pressed to find a straight, uninterrupted run between my two bases, wherever I chose to locate them.

The snails from both collection points would be marked, each sample with its own colour, and released in the centre of the tray. My hypothesis was that those snails from the Home area would sooner or later return to their own base, while the Away snails would also make their way back to their favourite haunt. Dave, my mentor, had suggested another part to the experiment. It would be interesting and useful to watch the direction in which the snails moved immediately after their release, to see if this correlated with the direction of their Home or Away base. If they streaked off eagerly, as if they knew exactly where they were going, and then sustained that trajectory until they arrived at their bases, this would add further weight to the homing theory. However, the experiment would still stand alone without this extra dimension.

By mid-morning, I was making good progress. Conditions were good – cool with a scattering of light showers – and I had a few spare hours.

At first, all I could find were a few empty shells – it looked as if the birds had had a feast that morning. But then I found fourteen Home snails in their usual place amid the day-lily leaves by the patio doors. I found twenty-six Away snails all in one place, hiding in the *Sisyrinchium striatum*, an evergreen plant like an iris, with sword-shaped leaves and small, cream-yellow flowers arranged in spikes. This was good news. But the plant was bang in the middle of the garden, which I had planned to establish as the testing area (the midway point). I decided to shorten the testing distance and have the release tray midway between the patio and the sisyrinchium, even though this was less than half the original planned distance (I had hoped to use the whole length of the garden). Twenty-six snails seemed too good a catch to miss.

These were the materials I used:

- 1 compass
- 1 tin tray, marked with a circle divided into 8 segments or compass points
- Lead pencil for marking exit points on tray
- Nail polish in two colours

- 14 Home snails
- 26 Away snails
- 2 large buckets, one each for Home and Away snails
- Steel tape measure
- Pen and notebook for recording variables, such as weather, and the progress of snails as released

'*I set about marking the Away snails and the Home snails . . .*' My diary entry for that day makes me sound methodical, as if I were in full control of the experimental procedure. The reality was anything but. My diary does not record the sweat and tears involved in the marking procedure. My buckets did not have lids – a serious oversight. Capturing the snails was easy enough; keeping them in one place while I marked their shells was another thing altogether. No sooner had I placed the buckets containing the unmarked snails on the workbench of my summer house, than they all made a dash for freedom. They slithered up the side of the bucket, ready to somersault over the rim. I quickly shoved them back again, hastily placing large flowerpot saucers over the top of each bucket. The saucers didn't quite fit – there was a snail-sized gap, which I missed seeing at the time. One by one, I extracted each of the fourteen Home snails and painted a blob of Desire maroon nail polish on the back of their shells. Now what to do with them? If I had popped each one straight back into its holding bucket, they would all have jostled together and climbed on one another's backs, ruining my handiwork. So I set them down on the wooden workbench to dry, while I turned my attention to the Away snails. By the time I had

My Devon garden

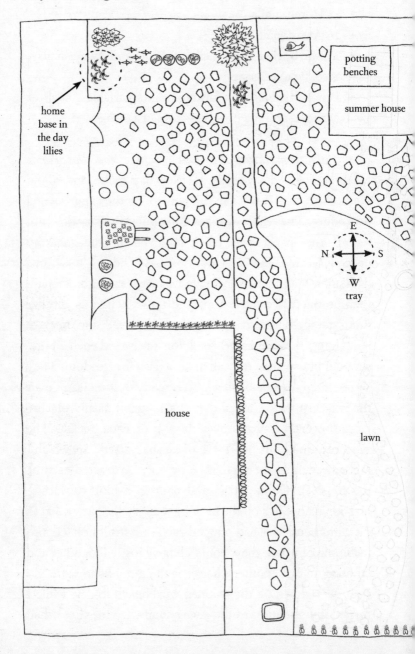

home base in the day lilies

potting benches

summer house

E
N ← → S
W
tray

house

lawn

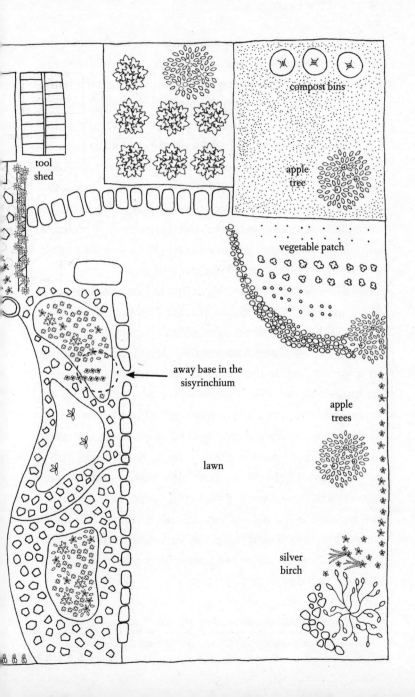

tool
shed

compost bins

apple
tree

vegetable patch

away base in the
sisyrinchium

apple
trees

lawn

silver
birch

begun to lift these out, a few at a time, to mark them, the maroon-spots had scattered far and wide. Some had sprinted towards a pot of sunflower seedlings; others legged it to the edge of the bench and were sliming down the sides towards freedom. Meanwhile, those crafty, unmarked snails that were still bucket-trapped had found the gap at the edge of the flowerpot saucer and, in an orderly line, were abseiling down the side of the container with the urgency of passengers sliding down the escape-chute of an aeroplane. The juveniles were the fastest, and were soon hiding under the bench and around the flowerpots and seed trays. Whoever said snails were slow? I could barely keep track of them.

I'd often heard the expression: 'It was like watching paint dry', but hadn't experienced until then how painfully slowly time could pass, when I was willing that nail polish to harden. The escaping Away snails were gleefully roaming far and wide, while their companions, still incarcerated in the bucket, peered over the rim to see what was going on, waiting their turn to slide to freedom. At last I rounded up all the Home snails and managed to corral them into their container, while I marked the remaining Away snails with a dot of yellow Sunburst. By now, all I wanted to do was lie down in a darkened room with a cold flannel over my brow, but the sun was up, and time was of the essence. If my snails got too hot, they would just go on strike and curl up in their shells, refusing to move for hours. So I got to work. My diary for that day continues:

I put all the snails in the centre of the tray. I watched to see in which direction they headed as they left the circle. As each

snail crossed the perimeter line, I noted, in a tally, whether
they were heading North, North-East, East, South-East, etc.

The snails were watched for two and a half hours to observe
behaviour, direction, progress, etc. By this time, 5 had
remained on the tray, others were spread out, some within
2 metres of the tray, others had gone further and disappeared.

Again, this cool scientific reportage does not portray the struggle I was having at this stage. The snails were moving at an incredible speed. I needed every ounce of concentration to keep up with them. While I was busy marking the exit point of one particular snail as it crossed the perimeter of the circle, and at the same time recording it in my notebook tally in the appropriate compass segment, another wilful gastropod had sneaked up to the opposite edge of the circle and was crossing the line. I needed four pairs of eyes, preferably at the end of tentacles, so that I could wave them round in all directions. I was fearful of missing some vital movement, the omission of which would ruin the experiment. With so many snails in my two samples, I should have asked someone to help me track them while I recorded their movements.

Another complication was that the resourceful creatures jumped on one another's backs to get a free ride. I'd see a pagoda of three wobbling over the perimeter of the circle at the same time. Was this cheating? Did it count as one, or three? How on earth was I supposed to record it? Finally, I decided that, to a mollusc's way of thinking, the end justified the means – this was obviously their preferred method of locomotion given the unusual circumstances they found themselves in. So I placed three crosses at the same exit point. Somehow, I managed to account for all of them, and afterwards felt absurdly pleased with myself.

My triumph, however, was short-lived. I had indeed duly recorded the exit points on the circle perimeter, and also in the appropriate tally column in my notebook. But what I had forgotten to do was to note whether each snail, as it exited, was a Home or Away snail. When I realised this omission, waking up in the dead of night, I was convinced that I had scuppered the experiment. It was only later, after worrying into the small hours, that I remembered it was an optional extra to note the initial direction each snail would choose to take. My mistake would not invalidate my results. Even so, I couldn't wait to do another experiment, as soon as possible, this time getting everything right.

Part of the scientific process is making observations about how an experiment has worked out, noting anything particularly striking or unusual. I was enjoying this part of the procedure. My snails were proving to be fascinating subjects.

In my diary, under the heading 'Observations', I noted how mesmerised I was by their speed – so fast that I could hardly keep up with them to do a tally, let alone a separate count of Home and Away snails. Watching their direction of travel generally, most were not decisive in the direction they chose, but I saw at least three Home snails heading off immediately in the exact direction of the Home base. Logically, a count of three out of fourteen snails was unremarkable on a statistical level, yet their movement seemed too purposeful to be just a coincidence.

By contrast, after two and a half hours, five of the snails had not moved at all. They were still curled up in their shells on the tray. Were they exhausted from repeatedly climbing up the side of the bucket and being shoved down again? As for those who decided on a quick getaway, their speed of locomotion appeared even faster than that of Archie, the champion snail. Could this be the subject for another experiment?

Many snails seemed disorientated, both at the point of release and as they left the tray. They climbed over one another and took time to choose a direction. Then they made searching movements, with much waving of tentacles. Three climbed up my leg – this had never happened to me before.

Why, I wondered, were so many snails in the sisyrinchium patch in the first place? There was no food there – the leaves were tough – so it was only a resting place, not a feeding place. This led me to question snails' hiding places generally. On what basis do they choose them? This might have implications for gardeners when they're choosing garden plants.

The next day, I made a triumphant entry in my diary:

Findings:
Action at last! 8 out of 14 snails from the Home patch were recovered in the Home patch, and 9 out of 26 snails from the Away patch were recovered in the Away patch. There was no crossover at all.

THIRTEEN

Home and Away

In the Devon lanes, tiered banks of wild flowers – celandine, primrose, red campion, sweet violet, bright blue speedwell – were framed by hedges of hawthorn and hazel, still in their first flush of delicate greenery. The apple and plum trees in my garden were still in blossom, and the blue-purple fronds of buddleja were attracting the first butterflies of the year. But, except for a tiny variety of tulip with striped leaves, most of the spring flowers had died down. In places, the earth looked bare, and I couldn't wait to fill the gaps with my carefully nurtured seedlings.

On a bench in the summer house (the only place in my garden that was safe from the merciless jaws of my snails), were trays of seedlings ready to plant out. There were sunflowers and sweet peas, lupins and African marigolds – all mollusc favourites. Then there were the vegetables: peas, lettuce and Swiss chard, and all varieties of climbing beans. I loved seeing them in their seed trays, looking so healthy. They reminded me of small children – full of boundless energy, their lives ready to unfold.

Every spring, I hated the task of pricking them out of their trays into pots. I had to decide which plant would live and which would die. This year, the drama ended the same way as ever – I crammed far too many into each pot. But once it was over, I felt relief. As I filled the pots with fresh compost, I began to enjoy myself.

This brief interlude, communing solely with my seedlings and largely ignoring the snails, had cleared my head. I approached the next experiment with renewed vigour. I was determined to get it right this time. But before I could even begin, I discovered a new problem. Snails don't conveniently hang about, patiently waiting in their various bases until they are needed. While most humans do a nine-to-fiver, coming back home to sleep at night, snails tend to do the opposite, livening up at night and going on the rampage in the vegetable patch. Moreover, their movements can vary widely according to the weather and temperature. Sometimes, they do behave rather like humans: a snail could go off exploring further afield than usual one day, hoping to sniff out a new restaurant. After a splendid meal, it might move on to a few more watering holes, meet some friends for a party and then bump into the partner of its wildest dreams. This could mean an overnight stay – or two – away from home on important business.

So two days later, I repeated the experiment. Because I could find so few snails – marked or unmarked – in the original Home patch, more Home snails were this time collected from another patch of lilies two metres nearer the Away base. So the total testing distance was eight metres instead of ten metres, with the testing tray at the midway point of four metres. The sample was much smaller: ten Home snails and eight Away snails.

Most of the snails collected in the Home and Away patches had already participated in the previous experiment two days ago, i.e. they had the same markings. These were the unadventurous – or lazy – ones that had decided to stay put for the day. (Before beginning, I had meticulously searched the whole garden to check that no late-arriving marked snails from the first experiment were heading home to confuse my results.) Only two new, unmarked snails had joined the Home snails' party, possibly using this patch as a stopover. I marked them in the same maroon. I wondered why there were so few new ones? Possibly, some had decided to find safer bases. Others could have been eaten by birds.

The experiment was carried out in the same way as previously, with the additional step of making separate counts of Home and Away snails as they left the direction-marked tray. For an hour I watched the snails closely to see where they were heading, hardly daring to look away from the testing area, let alone make myself a cup of tea. After that, I relaxed a bit and checked on them intermittently during the following four hours, at the same time as writing down some observations:

1. *As the snails left the tray, sliming out of the direction-marked segments of the circle, 3 of the Home snails showed*

a definite spurt of movement towards the Home base (as in the previous experiment). Their base lay due NNE, and the main cluster of exit points lay each side of this line, i.e. 4 going N, and 4 going NE. This was so definitive, it was quite spooky. Others clearly had their own agendas: 1 Home snail headed NW and 1 E. The Away snails, on the other hand, exited in a more random way, 2 going NW, 1 N, 1 E and 1 W. 2 stayed in the middle of the tray, curled up. (1 was unaccounted for.)

2. After a further hour, most of the Home snails had disappeared, whereas the Away snails had remained clustered round the tray or within 1 metre from it.

Later, a possible explanation for the way the Home snails seemed to beat such a determined path back to base occurred to me. The Away snails had their base four metres south of the testing tray, whereas the Home snails' camp was almost due north. Was it possible that there was some kind of magnetic pull, sensed through their skins, that was guiding them home so quickly? This idea is not as off-the-wall as it might sound: it is now thought possible that pigeons find their way home with the help of special receptors in their beaks that are sensitive to the magnetic field.

My diary for 20 May ended on a triumphant note:

Results!
8 Home snails were recovered from the Home patch.
6 Away snails were recovered from the Away patch;
1 was also found in the Home patch.

Conclusions:
I'm really excited about these results, which, although over a small area and with a small sample, seem very significant. Almost all the snails went back to their own bases, and there was an almost complete lack of crossover between the two.
NB The results from this experiment to be recorded on a data set.

My casual mention of having to record these results on a data set belies the panic I felt at finally having to approach my computer (Dave had let me off after the first experiment, although I had sent him the results). Data sets were scary kettles of fish, even after studying the template given to me by Dave. For the first time in my life, it was vital to be absolutely accurate in my recording – not easy for someone with my scatty brain – as well as making sure I clicked the right button on my screen. I was suddenly full of admiration for all those who naturally possessed a scientific mind, especially one that was wired up to computers. How much easier it must be to move through life logically, step by step, thinking things through systematically and unemotionally.

If my childhood heroine, Marie Curie, were alive today, she would have no problem with technology. In fact, she'd learn all the technicalities of word-processing, spreadsheets and desktop publishing in about five minutes, as well as installing, all by herself, the complicated software needed to analyse her results. Facebook would be a doddle. The point for me was that Mme Curie, in her quest to find radium, rose above difficulties and setbacks. She had a passion, and nothing would deflect her from her purpose. What could I, a humble amateur scientist, learn from such a heroine? Well, for a start, I could try not to be so terrified of my computer. It wasn't out to get me. It would not blow up in my face.

So, screwing my courage to the sticking-place, and fortified by dark chocolate and several cups of tea, I entered the results of my latest experiments on a data set. This is what the findings from my second instinct experiment looked like:

20 May 2010. Second experiment to prove homing instinct in Cornu aspersum, *the garden snail.*

10 Home snails were collected from the lily patch and 8 Away snails from the sisyrinchium patch. Home snails marked in maroon, Away snails marked in yellow. The testing distance was 8m, with the testing tray at the midway point, 4m.

Date of release	Dates of recovery	#Home snails returned to Home base	#Home snails crossed over to Away base	#Away snails returned to Away base	#Away snails crossed over to Home base	Weather conditions
2pm, 19 May						Very hot
	7pm, 20 May	8	0	6	1	Very hot, cooler pm

I had not expected my snails to scoot back so quickly to their Home bases. I'd anticipated many more entries under the 'Dates of recovery' heading, as they dribbled wearily back home one or two at a time. Finding those valiant creatures in the relative cool of the following evening curled up in their original places was a complete surprise. They had literally scorched home.

The next day, I was well rewarded for my efforts by an email from Dave, who had also posted a note on Facebook. It was headed 'Ruth's Amazing Data', and read:

To be honest, I'm flabbergasted by Ruth's results so far.

We've set up this 'Home' and 'Away' experiment for a very important reason. There is plenty of anecdotal evidence that a proportion of snails removed from a site will return to that site. But it's impossible to tell whether they return because it is their 'Home' or simply because 'Home' is the best patch of food for miles around. So, Ruth's experiment is designed to ask whether 'Home' snails are more likely to return to her patch of plants than snails collected from elsewhere ('Away' snails).

So far, so simple. Suddenly, Dave hit me with the hard-core science.

In scientific language, we have a null hypothesis and an alternative hypothesis.

Null hypothesis: Home snails are no more likely to go Home than Away snails.

Alternative hypothesis: Home snails are more likely to go Home than Away snails.

We can test our null hypothesis using a simple comparison of proportions.

In Ruth's first experiment, 8 Home snails were recovered,

all from the Home patch. 9 Away snails were recovered but none of them were in the Home patch. So we wish to compare 8/8 with 0/9. The probability of getting this result, if the null hypothesis is true, is only 1 in 10,000, or 0.01 per cent. So I think we can be confident in rejecting the null hypothesis. The snails in Ruth's first sample do indeed seem to have a homing instinct at short distance.

In Ruth's second experiment, 8 Home snails were recovered from the Home patch. 7 Away snails were recovered, but only one of them was found in the 'Home' patch. So we wish to compare 8/8 with 1/7. The probability of getting a result so biased in favour of the 'homing instinct' hypothesis, if the null hypothesis is true, is only 2 in 1,000, or 0.2 per cent. So, again, we can be confident in rejecting the null hypothesis. Ruth's second sample of snails also have a homing instinct at short distance.

We should note that many of the snails used in the second experiment were the same as those in the first. Maybe these are weird snails? It's important that Ruth continues her experiments with new snails, and tests for homing behaviour at greater distances between patches. Also, we're very keen that Ruth's fans try this at home.

Fantastic stuff!

I was thrilled with Dave's email, but there was one thing I didn't quite understand – those statistics. I knew they were based on probability, one of the few topics in maths that, unexpectedly, I had enjoyed as a child. It seemed to be all about the bad news and the good news – the chances of being struck by lightning or holding the winning Premium

Bond number. It sent my imagination spinning with fantastic tales. But the numbers in Dave's analysis were beyond me. How did they apply to our findings? If my snails *could* home, why were those numbers so small? Surely, they indicated that my molluscs had almost no chance of making it back to base. I rang him.

'Ruth,' Dave said. 'I want you to listen, absolutely quietly, for one whole minute. Don't interrupt. These results are based on something called Fisher's exact test, and I'm just about to explain it. Right?'

'Right.' I sat down and took a deep breath.

Dave explained that Fisher's exact test gives the probability of getting results by chance alone. In general, it was based on either a null hypothesis or an alternative hypothesis. As applied to our snail experiments, the null hypothesis was the assumption that snails are no more likely to travel home than to move away. The alternative hypothesis assumed the opposite: that snails do tend to move towards home. Our snail test was based on the null hypothesis, a crucial starting point that I had somehow missed, getting things totally the wrong way round. The numbers with all the noughts were the p-values – probability values. The tiny p-values that had so puzzled me actually confirmed homing instinct – rather than, as I had first thought, negating it.

So this was good news for my snails: their chances of sliming home were far, far better than mine were of ever winning the Lottery.

While I had been doing my experiments, something just as exciting had been happening on the University of Exeter's

Cornwall Campus. Under Dave's guidance, a third-year student, Sarah Ive, inspired by Dave's involvement in my research, had been carrying out two homing experiments, similar to mine but with much greater numbers. The first involved fifty-four Home and seventy-four Away snails over a distance of thirty metres. In the second, over a much shorter distance of eight metres, eighty-one Home and sixty-eight Away snails would be put through their paces. Dave's results, together with mine, would be announced at the final.

I'd love to be able to record that it was all plain sailing from now on. But I was on a rapid learning curve, not just about data sets, but also in relation to understanding the rollercoaster of triumphs and setbacks that every scientist has to navigate.

My third instinct experiment was, in terms of definitive results, a spectacular failure. Following Dave's advice, I wanted to prove my snails were not 'weird', as he had suggested they might be, but true homing creatures. With his guidance, I tried a different experiment, with one Home base, as before, but with as many different Away bases as I could find. In the end, I found three, and these would be the control areas.

On 22 May, I collected ten new, unmarked snails from the Home patch (the day lilies again). The Away snails came from a rockery in one corner of the back garden, the vegetable patch in another, and the strawberry bed against the house wall. These were as far apart from one another as possible, given the limited space. The average distance between the Home base and each of the three Away bases was, at 14.5 metres, almost double that of the previous experiment. I marked the snails in peacock blue, pink, emerald green and peach polishes. And this time, on top of the colour, I numbered each one with an indelible black fine liner. I also drew a rough sketch of the garden, superimposing a directional circle on top, with all the compass points marked. I noted all my collection points on the garden map, with a colour code and a brief description of where each group of snails had been found and the type of plants growing there. This should have been my most thorough and brilliant experiment so far.

Instead, it was a flop. After releasing them at noon, I attempted to recover them early the next day. I tried again the following day at 9am, and finally at 8pm.

Shock. Horror. No snails were recovered from any of the four patches (although one of the two Away snails from the rockery patch was found lurking in a place not even connected with the experiment). Therefore, only one out of twenty-five was recovered – a dismal, disappointing result.

So, what to think? Hypotheses:

1. The snails were collected on the hottest day of the year so far. The temperature remained high throughout the night. Therefore, locomotion could have been much slower as the snails' mucus dried out. This would have made them more vulnerable to birds.

2. They had had to cross a lawn – not as easy as the paving slabs in the first two experiments. So now terrain had become a variable.

3. Repeated disturbance, i.e. my probing fingers: being moved repeatedly could have led the snails to take fright and disappear into neighbouring gardens. I had noticed that the snails from the two previous experiments had found different, more sheltered, hiding places in their respective patches. For example, the Home snails in the day lilies on the patio had secreted themselves more deeply into adjacent stones and crevices.

I was beginning to feel sorry for my beleaguered back-garden snails.

The experiment was inconclusive. But now I had a set of variables to investigate.

'More research needs to be done!' This, I had now discovered, was the universal mantra of scientists in all fields. After a while, I felt less and less discouraged by my last failure. I still had plenty of time, and my brain was fizzing with ideas for new locations and distances.

Meanwhile, Michelle, the project manager of 'So You Want to be a Scientist?', had arranged some events. One was a talk, in which I explained my research, at Sparsholt College in Hampshire, which was hosting Radio 4's *Gardeners' Question Time*. Another was the launch of a new online experiment, the Great Snail Swap, whereby neighbours swapped snails to find out if homing instinct would guide them back to their original gardens and, if so, how far they would travel. For me, as an educationalist, the most important event would be the experiment piloted by my local school, St John's. All the children in Year 4 would bring samples of snails from their own gardens, mark them, release them in the playground and then see how long they took to find their way home.

This was turning out to be a most amazing summer. Every morning, I leapt out of bed with a new spring in my step, and could not wait to start the day. I was happier than I had been for a long time. Once more, I was doing the thing I most enjoyed: playing. And I was loving every minute of it.

FOURTEEN

The Learning Curve

Like many humans, snails are enthusiastic lovers, but have no parenting skills whatsoever. After laying their eggs, they bury them in the earth. Most snails choose damp, heavy soil in order to prevent the eggs, and their developing shells, from drying out. They use their tails to dig a hole and, after mixing the earth with mucus and excrement, they deposit the eggs in batches of thirty to fifty at a time. Larger species, such as my garden snails, can lay up to one hundred. But after this cursory and minimal act of parental involvement, the snail leaves its offspring alone, often resulting in their grisly ends.

They are now vulnerable to environmental conditions. Wind, blowing across the surface of the soil, can dry them out. Light rain is good, keeping the soil damp, but a heavy storm can wash the eggs up to the surface, rendering them vulnerable to predators. Frost has the same effect, causing deep fissures in the earth. Similarly, a prolonged hot spell dries out the earth – in my Devon clay, cracks soon appear, leaving the eggs widely exposed to sun damage. Predators include birds, ground beetles and small mammals. In my garden, the seagulls circling above in the early morning will eat anything that catches their eye. Because of the eggs' extreme vulnerability, only a small percentage survive – often as few as five per cent.

There might be a good reason behind the snail's apparently callous abandonment of its offspring. If the parent were to return again and again to check up on the eggs, perhaps to cover them up if they had become exposed, its trajectory towards the nest would leave slime trails. These silvery clues could lead straight to an easy meal for any hungry creature in the vicinity. Maybe snail parents are not as heartless as they seem.

The eggs are round, with a white calcareous shell. In some species, they are soft and transparent. Most hatch within six weeks, having generally been deposited in summer or autumn. Those laid in late autumn are often held in a state of suspended animation until the next spring, awaiting warmer weather. When digging over the soil in autumn, I have occasionally noticed a mass of tiny, opaquely white balls. Bunched together, they bear a slight resemblance to tapioca – my least favourite pudding at school.

Newly hatched babies look like miniature adults. Each already has a thin, fragile shell – the protoconch. This is secreted by glands within the embryo's mantle (a fold of skin that encloses the animal's gut) while it is still inside the egg. The protoconch forms the apex of the adult's shell – on close inspection, this sometimes appears to have a smoother and thinner surface than the rest of the structure. The shell then adds subsequent whorls, growing larger and giving its occupant more room for growth.

When they hatch, the babies eat their egg casings to obtain the calcium they need for shell manufacture. They have been known to eat those of their siblings, too, and even the siblings themselves, so vital is this ingredient. Snails reach full size within two to three years; mature animals can be identified by the lip that develops round the opening of their shells. Depending on weather and climate conditions, it can take two to six years for a snail to become sexually mature enough to reproduce and begin the cycle again.

I was glad to observe that the parents of Year 4 children at St John's had far better parenting skills than my snails. All had conscientiously sent their children to school with lunch boxes. Each contained, not sandwiches and crisps, but a collection of snails, which were happily munching through their own lunches of lettuce and cabbage leaves. These gallant pioneers in the first-ever schools homing experiment had been collected from the pupils' gardens – no doubt with a lot of prompting and help from the grown-ups.

Thirty excited eight- and nine-year-olds bounced out into the enclosed playground where the snails were to be released. Most pupils lived within half a mile from the school, a few even nearer. All of them were absolutely certain that their own snails would find their way back home. Equally confident of success were the two children who lived much further afield, one in Buckfastleigh and the other in Torquay – respective distances of eight and twelve miles. They had no doubt at all that their one-footed travellers could navigate seashores and riverbanks, main roads and shopping centres.

Before the day's experiment, Rachel Azzopardi, the class teacher, had explained the concepts of homing and direction. The pupils understood how to use a compass. Miss Azzopardi had enlarged a map of the neighbourhood, and this was displayed on the classroom wall, with all the children's homes marked on it to give them a good idea of how far, in metres and kilometres, their homes were from the school. The snails' progress – i.e. any mollusc sightings between the school and the pupils' homes – would be plotted on the map, so even if the creatures could not quite manage the whole distance, the pupils could measure the success of their own sample, compared to that of their classmates. Tracking how far their own snails had managed to travel from their release point would be a learning experience in itself.

In their exercise books, the children had written up all the stages of the experiment: capture, marking, release, etc. Miss Azzopardi had given them background information: they knew how snails moved along on their own rivers of slime, and their favourite diet and hiding places. She had devised a nifty data set with column headings: child's name; number of snails in the sample; colour and design of markings; direction of home; compass direction favoured when leaving the testing area. The markings were striking and novel – and probably unknown in the history of mollusc research. The children had painted their snails' shells in yellow, blue, red or pink, then decorated them with a variety of shapes and designs. Crosses, circles, dots and lines, painted onto brightly coloured shells, stood out against the grey Tarmac as the children, in groups of three or four, released their snails in chalk circles marked with all the compass directions.

It was blazingly hot; easily the hottest day of the year so far. The playground, an area half the size of a tennis court, sizzled – and so did the snails. The testing circles ranged round the edges; even so, to reach the nearest patch of grass or shade, the snails had to travel a metre or two. Some clearly hadn't a clue where they were, and started off towards the centre of the Tarmac. This created chaos, as the pupils rushed around to see how their friends – both mollusc and human – were getting on. Two children had been given the very important job of 'cooler', and ran around with watering cans, dousing Tarmac, snails and one another. Even so, the hot, sticky surface dried in the blink of an eye. Snails, children, teachers, assistants and parent helpers sweltered together, but I was seriously worried about the fate of the snails. Michelle, who was recording the experiment for *Material World*, circulated with her microphone, calm and efficient as ever, capturing the excitement. Everywhere was movement and noise.

'Whoops! I've squished it – sorry,' was the anguished cry of one pupil, as he accidentally trod on one of the escaping gastropods.

The children watched, entranced, as their little charges hot-footed it out of the circle, most of them hell-bent on getting off the burning surface. Frankly, releasing snails on Tarmac on the hottest day of the year was not the best start to an experiment.

The youngsters were fascinated to see how some snails piggybacked whenever they could, while others seemed to have thrown in the sponge and were curled up in their shells to conserve energy. In each group, one child had been appointed to record the direction of travel. During the following days and weeks, as they walked home each night with their parents, all the children would keep an eye out, not only for their own snails, but for those of their class-mates, too. In their playtime, and before and after school, they would search the playground and just beyond the boundary fences, reporting back to their teacher, who would plot each snail's position, with the date, on the classroom map.

In two of the groups, the children reported a definite initial movement towards home. In one of these two groups, it was possible that the snails were just desperate to reach nearby shade. In the other, however, there was no cover at all to account for such a determined trajectory towards home.

As they left their circles, the snails' movement became more random. Soon the playground was a bustling concourse. The snails spread out far and wide, tiny beacons on the shimmering, sun-baked Tarmac.

The behaviour of the pupils was as interesting to me as that of the snails. All of them were fully concentrating and excited. Biology and anatomy, ecology and habitat, maths and measurement, geography and orientation – all were an intrinsic part of the experiment, absorbed in an effortless and joyful way. The children were also cooperating with one another fully. Not only was this a scientific experiment, it was a successful educational one, too.

To me, the whole afternoon was a prime example of the 'outdoor classroom' in operation, a concept that science educationalists have long been advocating. In such an environment, children can learn more in the space of an hour than in a whole day of desk-based study. I could see that even the most fidgety children were fully engaged. They were doing what comes most easily to eight- and nine-year-olds – playing, and moving their bodies energetically. It is simply not natural for children of this age to sit still for long periods.

I wished that I could conjure up a magic carpet, and transport to this playground all the grey-suited policymakers in governments past and present, all those grim-faced, joyless bureaucrats who continually devise restrictive tests and complicated changes to the curriculum that heap stress upon teachers and constrain a child's capacity to learn. Then they would see true education happening before their eyes. At primary level, children have a wonderful curiosity about the world. They learn best by doing, and to exploit this fully, they must have more time for hands-on experiences. How else can we foster our future scientists?

There was another experiment to be done at home. This was a pilot for the nationwide Great Snail Swap. My next-door neighbour, Bruce, helped by his young son, Peter, were the trailblazers. We each collected a number of snails from our front gardens – I was giving my poor back-garden molluscs a well-earned rest. I found mine in cracks and crevices in the rockery next to the pond; Bruce and Peter burrowed about in a huge clump of crocosmia that had spread over a wide area of their garden. The two locations were nine metres apart, with the fence in between. The experiment would be much more straightforward than previous ones. We still wanted to confirm that the snails from each of our gardens would return to their original patches, but now the emphasis was on how far they could travel to do so. So there was no need for a midway testing area. The fence that divided our two properties, rather than presenting a problem because it got in the way, would become a variable – a barrier – to be accounted for alongside all the other variables, such as weather and terrain.

The snails were marked with nail polish, blue for mine, purple for Bruce's, then placed in two large, separate flowerpots, marked A and B. Then, in true neighbourly style, Bruce, Peter and I met at the garden fence. Flowerpots were solemnly exchanged. During the next few days, we would watch the snails' progress. Might they get so homesick that they would beat a hasty retreat back to their own bases, or – treacherous creatures – decide that they preferred their neighbours' garden? Perhaps they would default on the experiment altogether and go on a long vacation elsewhere.

Neighbours and friends all over the country were encouraged to participate in this citizen science. A few days later, the online questionnaire appeared on the BBC website. It was easy enough to complete – even I could do it. A series of drop-down menus presented options: date of release, distance between the two properties, weather conditions, number of snails in each sample, barriers the snails had to cross (walls, fences, roads, streams, buildings) and, finally, the date they returned. I hoped fervently that hundreds, even thousands of listeners to *Material World* would be fired with the spirit of scientific enquiry. This experiment would provide the most comprehensive survey ever undertaken of homing ability and distance, as well as snail behaviour under different conditions. Dave, with his team of statisticians, had the challenging task of analysing the results. I couldn't wait for all the responses to come flooding in.

I was well stuck into the homing project when two intriguing scientific papers popped through my letterbox. Previously, I had hunted unsuccessfully on the Internet and through library records for research into the homing instinct of snails (even though I had found many papers on homing instinct in limpets). Dave, my mentor, was more practised at delving into the dusty recesses of scientific record. He produced two studies relating to homing in snails – the most recent was thirty-eight years old.

The first was a Californian study by D. C. Potts, entitled 'Persistence and Extinction of Local Populations of the

Garden Snail *Helix aspersa* in Unfavorable Environments' (1975). It focused on the conditions that favoured snail growth in three different, uncultivated habitats, studying population sizes and changes in these locations. One observation jumped out from the page: Potts noted that 'migration between neighboring populations was minimal because the snails have strong homing tendencies'. The author recorded finding snails on the same bush, or clumps of bushes, for months or years on end. Potts hypothesised that the restricted dispersal of *Cornu aspersum* (or *Helix aspersa*, as it was then known) was probably caused by individuals returning to their original locations after each night's activity, and that this homing behaviour seemed to involve attachment to a general area, rather than to the specific resting sites that had been described in Europe by a much earlier researcher (J. W. Taylor, in studies carried out between 1894 and 1921).

So Potts had started with the very clear assumption that snails could make their way home. This was highly relevant to our own research, even though the article was concerned with other aspects of snail behaviour. I was also intrigued to see that Potts referred to research that had been carried out more than a hundred years ago. Although Potts had referred only briefly to Taylor's theory that snails were faithful to their resting sites (and I was unable to follow this up because Taylor's original paper was unobtainable), I was delighted that Dave and I were following in such historical footsteps.

The second article, by Carl Edelstam and Carina Palmer from the Department of Zoology, University of Stockholm, was entitled 'Homing Behaviour in Gastropods' (1950).

The subject was *Helix pomatia*, the Roman snail, rather than *Cornu aspersum*, but there are many similarities between the two species. Its aim was primarily to gather data for an ecological study of a particular snail population in a suburban Stockholm garden. In the spring of 1949, the researchers marked with ink all adult Roman snails found in the garden, a total of sixty-eight, and immediately released them. The garden was carefully searched on 1 July, 1 August and 1 September. Forty-five of the originals were recovered close to the collecting area.

This first experiment was followed up by some field experiments, investigating movements of snails over a forty-eight-hour period in five different locations across Stockholm. In each one, the researchers released groups of snails that they had collected from several small, well-defined areas lying in different directions from the release point. The diagrams and maps were all hand-drawn – no fancy computer software in 1950 – yet they were clear and easy to understand. One of the selected places was a woodland, in which forty-three snails were collected from three different bases, then released. After two days, thirty snails were recovered, most of which showed marked directional movement back towards their respective bases.

What struck me most about these field experiments was the method used. The researchers stated that to 'test the strength and precision of homing under unbiased conditions . . . we took care that the immediate surroundings of the releasing point should be flat and also tolerably uniform with regard to light and shadow, humidity, and exposure to wind'. They also wanted to ensure 'that the releasing point as well as its surroundings in several directions should be a suitable habitat for the snails, so that they had no immediate reason for moving or, if they did move, to prefer one direction to another'.

This differed from our method of releasing snails in a neutral, midway spot that might not be to their liking – perhaps our snails had more incentive to find their way home. If only we had more time, I would have loved to replicate our own experiments with the above difference in procedure. But I didn't think Dave would be too enthusiastic – he was fully stretched analysing our results so far. Mind you, for the purposes of originality, I was relieved that we were going about our experiments in a different way.

Another intriguing test was done to find out how long it would take the snails to home if they had been moved repeatedly. In an extraordinary experiment: 'seventy-three snails, having been used during four days for long-distance trials in habitats rather different from their own, and later kept for two days in bags in a town flat, were released at a point 25–45 metres from the place where they were first collected . . . about half the specimens – but not necessarily more – [have] retained their full homing capacity even after such adversities, whereas the others (at least a few, possibly half the total) have lost it.'

Guiltily, I thought of my snails. They, too, had suffered 'adversities' in my garden. I hadn't kept them indoors in a bag for two days, but I had repeatedly moved the 'used' ones, picking them up when they were having a well-earned snooze and conscripting them into a new experiment. However, for me, what was most significant about this

Swedish study was that half the snails appeared to know how to find their way home, even after being cooped up for two days in a town flat.

One of the researchers' fascinating conclusions was that 'homing ability ceases completely somewhere between 150 and 2,000 metres'. This meant that the snails I had been taking regularly to the woodland, a quarter of a mile away, were unlikely to return. I could not decide whether I was pleased or sorry. I'd been careful to relocate them in a safe place, where they would be happy and settle down, yet, at the same time, I longed to see them romping home from such a grand distance. What a great day in the annals of mollusc history that would have been!

The researchers also speculated as to which senses guide the snails home. They ruled out sight and hearing, as well as touch and taste. The conclusion was that smell was the determining factor, and if snails were downwind, scents were picked up much more easily. Crucially, the researchers remarked that if smell were accepted as the guiding factor, one also had to accept the existence of a persistent memory related to certain scents. This was no surprise to me at all. I had known all along that snails were far more intelligent than anyone believed.

I had so much to learn from such meticulously executed experiments. Displacement and disturbance, for example. I had already moved my snails about a lot while doing the instinct experiments. Maybe if, after their first homing, I were deliberately to displace them once more, I could find out if they still had the stamina and determination to slog home yet again. *If they possessed the memory to do so!* The idea that snails had a memory intrigued me. Could I do a different, long-term experiment, I wondered, allowing my epicurean gastropods to make their homes in the midst of various scented delicacies, then taking them away to see if they would return there season after season? So many experiments, so little time!

I wondered how far the snails in the St John's experiment were wandering at this very moment. Had they given up just outside the school gates, or were a few stalwarts creeping through hedges and grass verges, round garages and over walls, to feast once more on their beloved garden plants? I was eagerly awaiting the results of the Great Snail Swap, too. My snails – and my neighbour's – had only to travel nine metres, but I reckoned that other people, living further apart, would have spectacular results to report. I needed to coax another neighbour into snail swapping. Who on earth could I ask? Most people in my road spent their time zapping molluscs, rather than playing silly games with them. How could I persuade them to call a ceasefire in their war against snails?

FIFTEEN

Misadventures Galore

Dave had urged me to do as many instinct experiments as possible, to add to our growing body of evidence that snails have a natural homing ability. I knew that he was still sceptical about what was actually going on in their mollusc brains. Was it really a determined intention to get home, or were they like drunken creatures, lurching about round town until by happy chance they found themselves outside their own front door and thought: 'Hmm, thith lookth familiar'?

I felt that I had exhausted the snails in my own garden. I needed to find some new snails, belonging to someone who liked them and was interested in their welfare (and who did not think that I was entirely batty – by now, my reputation as 'that mad snail lady' was spreading throughout the town).

As so often happens, the person I was seeking lived right under my nose – more exactly, just across the road. My neighbour Sue loves all creatures great and small, including snails. When I moved into my house in 1994, Sue was contentedly installed in her own home with a menagerie of pets. At one point, twenty-three rabbits occupied hutches that spilled out from her kitchen door into the garden, sheltered from the weather by a covered way. For ten years, nine cats patrolled her front garden and the end of the road. Sue has now downsized to four rabbits, four guinea pigs and two cats. A couple of lovebirds and a pair of budgies sing and squawk in their living-room cages, competing with human chit-chat and the television.

For many years, Sue was vice-chair of an animal shelter. Her duties included home visits. After giving the cat or dog a decent interval to adapt to its new owners and environment, she would call round to see if it had settled in well. If the animal slunk around, tail down, avoiding its new owners, or would never emerge from under the settee, she knew that it was unhappy. The tales she tells are often heart-rending. Sue's reputation for rescue and care was spreading, and a few people were beginning to take advantage of her. Once, she came home from work to find a very sick cat stretched out on her doorstep. It was so weak that it could not stand up, and had to be carried into the house. It was obvious that the animal, far too ill to walk, had been callously dumped.

I knew that Sue would help me, but first I needed to reassure her that, in the course of these experiments, not a single animal would be harmed.

It was raining steadily as, late one afternoon in mid-July, I gathered snails from two separate areas of Sue's front garden – homing-instinct experiment number four was about to get under way. This would be carried out in exactly the same way as the previous three instinct experiments, with the midway testing tray. Our purpose was to gather as much definitive evidence as possible to support our theory that snails could find their way home. Sue kept me under close surveillance, in between feeding the rabbits, checking to see that I placed the snails gently, shell-side up, in their collection pots and kept them fed on a gourmet diet. My plan had been to release them immediately after marking them, when they were most likely to be mobile. The rain would have helped the snails, but for me it was a stumbling block, preventing me from marking their progress in my notebook.

I needed to wait until the rain stopped. This looked unlikely to happen that day, so all the snails needed to be kept somewhere overnight. I took them back home and placed them by my shed, covering the pots with a saucer that, this time, fitted exactly. I checked everything – breathing holes and a choice menu for their breakfast. I half expected Sue to creep over at midnight and do a home visit. During the night, the rain lashed down, and strong winds howled round the house. In the morning, I found one of the containers overturned, its contents scattered far and wide. All the Away snails had made a bolt for it – much to Sue's delight and amusement.

That afternoon, 16 July, it was cool and sunny with some cloud; the conditions were right. Carefully, I carried the Home snails, still behaving themselves in their pot, back over the road to Sue's front garden, where the experiment was to take place. Now, there was just the small matter of replacing the bolted Away snails with another bunch of unsuspecting victims. I feared that, by this time, Sue's garden, like mine, would be running out of snails. But we discovered many more with no effort at all; her garden was clearly snail heaven.

At last, the experiment went ahead. Once again, the area available was a limiting factor and I had to be content with another testing distance of nine metres. The Home patch was a clump of rock-loving plants that grew at the base of the sunny, south-facing wall of the house. The Away patch, from which we had just collected our newest recruits, was, by coincidence, another clump of crocosmia lying to the west. I had sketched a map of the garden on a sheet of paper so that I could plot the trajectory of each snail as it left the testing circle.

We marked the eight Home snails in Sparkly Pink wet shine. Secretly, I longed to try the Sparkly Pink out on my fingernails, but it was too bright and flashy. Normally, that would apply to the snails, too – the shell would attract predators, shining out like a beam from a lighthouse. But now, with Sue on the case, I had no worries on that score – she would be watching out for them like a hawk. I just had to trust that her heart wouldn't melt if she saw a family of hungry mice, and turn a blind eye to the fate of the molluscs.

Both groups were carefully numbered. The ten Away snails were blobbed with white marking fluid, onto which I now realised that numbers could be written more easily with a fine black felt-tip pen. Ideally, I would have liked to mark all my samples in this way, but by now I had too many experiments going on at the same time. Different-coloured nail polishes were the only way to distinguish between them.

After release, the Home snails set off rapidly and purposefully towards their base. The Away snails dithered; they moved more slowly and their direction was more scattered. I wondered whether this was because the crocosmia, the resting site that gave them shelter and shade but no food (I've never seen any nibbled leaves), was not their priority. They were very hungry, and were trying to reorient themselves in order to find a meal. Remarkably, as in all the experiments so far, many Home snails scooted north, as if there was some magnetic pull controlling them. But because all my testing distances so far had run north to south, with Home base at the north, this didn't prove anything – yet.

After just over an hour, three out of the eight Home snails had already arrived back at their base. A fourth was dithering, sliming through the grass between north and north-east. The other four were spread out more randomly, but still contained within the north and east sectors. This angle of dispersion definitely suggested a deliberate movement, rather than a drunken lurch. As with all my experiments, the snails would have to be carefully monitored throughout the following days, until the final results were entered on my spreadsheet.

What struck me most was how swiftly the snails were moving. For a long time, I had wondered how fast they could go. Findings varied widely. For example, a speed of three to five metres per day (in wet weather) had been mentioned in the Swedish study I had just read. To me, this seemed ridiculously slow. At this very moment, between the grass and Sue's house wall (about a metre), a spirited juvenile was streaking home at a startling rate. This was my chance.

Using a steel tape, I measured a distance of fifty centimetres. Starting at zero, the snail crawled briskly along its length until, with a celebratory wave of its tentacles, it reached the finish and disappeared off the end of the tape into the plants by the wall. Timed with a stopwatch, this athletic sprint took exactly six minutes. It worked out at five metres per hour, not per day. I had taken a photo of the snail in action, just to remind myself that this impressive feat had actually happened – this arose from the almost pathological belt-and-braces approach that I had developed towards my experiments. I was well aware of a natural and understandable instinct in all types of research: in his or her eagerness to make the findings fit the hypothesis, the researcher may not 'see' a vital occurrence or piece of information or, quite unconsciously, might select only those facts that support the theory, ignoring any contradictions. I was alert to the danger of falling into that trap. This was where I needed a witness – Sue was watching this speed experiment very closely, although I suspected that she was far more concerned about the snail's risk of overexerting itself than whether or not I was cheating. I knew that she would not relax one iota until all the creatures had returned safely to their homes.

In all my experiments, I had to keep in mind their practical application, particularly for gardeners. Knowing how fast snails could travel would help us to gauge how far to take them away, and how much time to allow for their return. It also had implications for how long the mettlesome molluscs from the Great Snail Swap and the school experiment would take. One of the pupils at St John's lived in Torquay, a distance of twelve miles. My young champion would struggle to keep up its pace of five metres per hour for days or even months on end. Even shorter distances would be a challenge. Allowing, say, twelve hours in every twenty-four for resting and feeding, some snails might, in theory, manage sixty metres per day. But we would also have to allow for ground surface, obstacles, barriers and extremely hot weather.

I was tremendously relieved that not a single snail in Sue's garden had been crushed, bird-snatched or had a heart attack. I wanted Sue to help me again. Following up the experiment with my neighbour Bruce, I needed to do another snail swap, this time over a longer distance. However, this one was fraught with danger. In order to get back to their respective homes, our snails would have to creep to the end of our gardens, slither under hedges and – horror of horrors – cross the road, the turning circle at the end of our cul-de-sac. When I broached the idea to Sue, she visibly blanched, and reminded me about the toads, which, every February and March, stride up the road in platoons at dusk, making for my pond. Unsuspecting motorists often drive over these poor creatures. Other than standing on guard all night, there is not much that anyone can do. I had to convince Sue that our snails would not meet a similar fate.

I collected eleven snails from the rockery in my front garden, and marked them in pale apricot Bonbon. I reckoned this muted colour would not attract birds, nor any curious children that, during the day, would be playing at the end of the cul-de-sac. Sue marked the seven snails that she found in a clump of tall grasses using sky-blue Aqua Cool for the same reason. This time, the distance between the two locations was an impressive 21.5 metres. After being swapped, for an hour the snails remained immobile. I went home and had a meal before returning to Sue's garden. They had all vanished. It was disappointing not to be able to track their direction, but Sue was much happier, as none appeared to have ventured out into the road. Relieved, she went off to feed her rabbits.

Three days later, I went out snail spotting, hoping to find some in the road, alive and well. It was warm and muggy, the end of a perfect summer evening. Throughout June, and right up to now in mid-July, the weather had been very hot. In my garden, the earth was cracked and dry. I could just about manage to keep my vegetables alive by frequent watering from my two rain barrels, but they were almost empty, and I disliked using tap water. As for the flowers, only the sun-loving geraniums looked happy in their dry pots.

No marked snails were about, either in the road or anywhere else, nor had any been spotted recently. They must all have retreated into the nearest damp haven, inside flowerpots and in cool cracks and crevices. Instead, lots of new snails had replaced the experiment snails. The more times I checked, the fewer snails I found, even in the shadiest places. This confirmed my suspicions. These experimental subjects had become sensitised to disturbance and were so disgusted by such treatment in their own garden that they had upped sticks and relocated to a safer and more peaceful home.

The thorny issue of variables was coming up again and again, and the question of disturbance was bothering me the most. I would have loved to set up a controlled experiment to prove its effect. This is what I would do: collect two lots of snails, each marked in a different colour, from two different locations in a very long garden, much bigger than mine. These locations would be matched exactly for the type of flowers or vegetables, sun or shade levels, north– south orientation and any other variable I could think of. The two collection areas would have to be a long way from other juicy plants to eliminate the chance of the snails being attracted to new delicacies. They would be released from a central position. First, I would wait until several snails had returned to each base. I would choose one of the two locations to leave undisturbed for a given period, say, two weeks. The other location would be searched every day. At the end of this period, I would check to see if the undis- turbed location had a greater population, thus confirming my hypothesis.

Logistically, this experiment wasn't possible in my own garden, unless I dug up my meagre patches of lawn to create two identical flower beds. Anyway, I did not have the time: I was trying to cram a whole lifetime of research into five precious months.

Nevertheless, a long, uninterrupted testing area without barriers was still my Holy Grail. I was keen to do another instinct experiment, but over a much longer distance, where the only variables would be weather conditions, time of day and temperature. I needed to borrow a massive garden, just for a week or two. Once more I was in luck. I happened to know someone who had just such an expanse of ground. I had first met Carole when, for a brief item on the local news, she had come round to film me doing the experiments. Cheekily, I had asked her the size of her garden, storing the information up for future use. Even more cheekily, I now asked her if I could borrow it for a while, and to my delight she agreed. Her garden was a real humdinger. More than an acre in size, it bordered open fields and farmland. Leading off a large central lawn, secret paths led between small clumps of woodland, and open spaces disappeared beyond grassy slopes and emerged as small, hidden dips revealing a summer house or chicken coop. It was too easy to become distracted – all I wanted to do was to explore.

The testing area for my fifth instinct experiment was ideal – thirty metres separated the two collection bases. At one end of the huge stretch of lawn was an enormous pond surrounded by rocks and water-loving plants. Here, I found some snails clinging to the underside of stones. At the other end, a long rockery surrounded the patio, where there were many more snails hiding in the cool crevices, grouped together in colonies. Setting out the testing equipment proved to be a challenge. I was 'helped' by the family's retriever, which exuberantly grabbed various bits of the experiment as soon as I turned my back. But Carole's two young daughters, together with a school friend, proved to be highly competent assistants. They marked and numbered all the snails carefully and neatly, then helped me to record their progress after they were released.

In spite of the garden's many advantages, the results from this experiment were very disappointing. No snails returned home. Carole and the children kept an eye out, and I went back the following day and every day after that. All I found were dry, empty shells and a few dried-out specimens. But these were not the snails from my experiment: they were unmarked, and discovered in hidden places well away from the collection areas, so I concluded that they had died previously, from natural causes. There was no doubt that the dry summer had affected the existing population. Soon, I had to admit defeat. The snails had all scarpered, except for one. This unfortunate Away snail, only just alive, had a huge hole in its shell. This damage suggested predators. Who were they, and where were they coming from?

Carole's garden was perfect in so many ways, but in my eagerness for a large area, I had ignored another important variable. I'd overlooked the significance of its location, right next to open countryside and farmland. This was the habitat of small mammals – shrews, mice and rats – as well as birds. To keep them out, the whole testing area would have to be protected in some way, from above with netting and below ground with some kind of fine wire mesh, just below the surface of the grass – an impossible task. Would it ever be possible, I wondered for the umpteenth time, to find a perfect testing ground, one where my snails could travel unimpeded?

The methods that predators employ to unpack their snail breakfasts are highly inventive. The murder weapon and means of destruction are usually plain to see, revealing the identity of the perpetrator. Birds, particularly thrushes, smash the shell repeatedly against a stone, using it as an anvil. As I had noticed in my childhood, one song thrush will have its favourite stone and use it again and again, surrounding it with broken, empty shells. Other birds eat the eggs, or unprotected babies, if they become uncovered. Larger snails provide tasty meat for bigger species of bird, which use their beaks to smash the shell, swallowing some of it together with the flesh. In these cases, the snail is not always completely digested. Tiny bits of shell encased in droppings beneath the bird's nest will point to the culprit.

Small mammals, such as field mice and hedgehogs, nibble at the shell. Moles and rats, voles and shrews hunt by night, and I reckoned that this was when most of my experiment disappeared. Carole's garden was a perfect hunting ground for the creatures that lived just outside its boundaries. I had somehow managed not to anticipate that the open countryside would present such a problem. Other predators lived on site. One day, while poking about in the rockery, I heard an unmistakable clucking behind me. I whirled round to see a group of chickens trailing after me, watching my every move. Cloaked in feathers of every possible shade of russet, brown and orange, these were beautiful, proud creatures, no two the same. They were on the prowl, and I would lead them to their next meal. Who could blame them? This was their garden, after all.

By contrast, I had always considered snails to be fairly peaceable creatures. So I was shocked to learn that some attack one another. The rosy wolfsnail (*Euglandina rosea*) is a bruiser of a mollusc. Its shell alone can be as long as seven centimetres. This native of Florida, which has spread to other southern US states, was introduced into Hawaii, Papua New Guinea and Bermuda to control giant African land snails, a crop pest. Also known as the cannibal snail, it has decided that it most fancies other, smaller snails, and often swallows them whole. The decollate snail (*Rumina decollata*), which comes from the Mediterranean, is a particular threat to garden snails (fortunately not here in Britain). Studies have found that it eats them from the inside out. Indeed, many gardeners abroad have begun introducing it deliberately to control *Cornu aspersum*. I was most upset by this discovery, not just because of the horrible fate of my favourite species of snail. When upholding 'snail rights' to anyone who would listen for a nanosecond, my most persuasive argument had always been that snails, whatever else they get up to, do not kill one another.

However, many have found ingenious ways to avoid being attacked. Some use camouflage. The land snail *Merdigera obscura* covers its shell with materials gathered from the environment. Occurring most in immature snails, this camouflage varies from mud particles to small fragments of lichen, and the outer layer of its shell resembles a little knot on the bark of a tree. Other molluscs have found ways to defend themselves when under attack. Some slugs jettison their tails. The garlic glass snail (*Oxychilus alliarius*) gives off a garlic smell that repels hedgehogs and other predators.

As if snails didn't have enough to contend with already, constantly under attack by birds, small mammals and cannibalistic cousins, we humans add to their problems. Our ancestors were great mollusc-munchers. In most parts of the world, empty shells, heaped together in piles, have been found by archaeologists. Today, we are not quite so enthusiastic about land snails, although it is a curious fact that most people are comfortable with the idea of eating shellfish. The very idea of ingesting a slimy snail (even though its slime will long have disappeared by the time it reaches the table), let alone having first to winkle it out of its shell, fills most British folk with utter repugnance. Yet our nearest European neighbours have no such reservations. Roman snails are one of France's most traditional dishes.

The French also eat the smaller garden snail, known as *petit gris*. In Britain, there are farms that rear both species for the table. But even those minority gourmands who might try snails in restaurants are put off cooking them at home by the long, drawn-out preparation required. The snails must first be purged of their excrement, so need to be starved for several days or be fed on a restricted diet. And, of course, they have to be killed and the shells removed by popping them into boiling water.

Once, while on holiday in France many years ago, I tried *petit gris*. Their rubbery texture, and the monotony of having to wade through twenty-four of them on my plate, did not appeal. But as an old French friend used to say, '*Il ne faut pas disputer ni les couleurs ni les goûts,*' which, roughly translated, means that there's absolutely no point in arguing about what colour people say they are seeing, or about their tastes. We perceive the world through our senses, as well as our reason, and each one of us views the world in our own unique way. I know someone who is a great advocate of fresh roadkill. The remains of deer, rabbit and hare have all graced his table. I haven't asked him about cats and dogs. This man's meat is my poison, yet I respect his right to act in accordance with his own world view: if he doesn't eat it, it will either rot or be eaten by another animal. He is not harming another creature. I am convinced, however, that snails will never be part of my diet – unless, due to some cataclysmic disaster, I find myself cast away from normal civilisation. Even then, I'm not sure that I could bring myself to throw my garden friends into the cooking pot.

Snail-munchers may be in the minority, but the bottom line is that most humans will stop at nothing to eliminate snails from their gardens by fair means or foul. Contemplating this fact brought me right back to my experiments. This was not simply research for its own sake. I wanted to demonstrate that there were kind ways to deal with our snails – ways that actually worked.

SIXTEEN

Chucking Snails

t was midnight. Crab-walking on my hands and feet round and round the turning circle at the end of my cul-de-sac, I peered down at the road. A persistent rain dripped off the end of my nose. The harsh light of the street lamp was a hindrance, rather than a help. It sucked the colour out of everything, making my mission almost impossible.

A heavily built middle-aged man appeared, leading a gambolling Alsatian. Seeing me, he stopped.

'You all right, love?'

'Yes, thank you,' I said, firmly. I wanted him to go – quickly. 'I'm fine. Just – just looking for something.'

'Ah!' I heard the relief in his voice. 'Dropped your keys, have you? I've done that. Infuriating, isn't it? Here, let me help you.'

He advanced towards me, smiling.

'No!' I shrieked, glancing down at his feet, encased in heavy boots, size 12s at least. Dangerous. 'No, I'm better off on my own, thank you.'

His smile froze. He looked bewildered and a bit hurt.

'It's because of your feet,' I said, by way of explanation.

Alarmed, he looked down. 'My *feet*? Why, what's wrong with them?'

'Nothing. But – it's the snails, you see. They're all over the road – and the pavement, too. Look,' I pointed a sweeping finger round the Tarmac. 'Millions of them!'

The man looked. At least fifty snails were sliming round without purpose, all going in different directions.

'So . . .' His voice trailed off uncertainly.

'So,' I rushed on. 'I'm looking for them.'

He scratched his head, frowning at me doubtfully. 'You're *looking* for them? But you can't have lost them. They're there!'

'It's *particular* snails I'm after,' I explained. 'They're *my* snails, you see.'

'Yours? You keep them as pets, then?'

'No. When I say they're mine, I mean they've got my markings. Apricot Bonbon.'

The man blinked, and took a step back onto the pavement. There was a horrible crunch under his foot. For a moment, he stared at me. Then, he reached out and clipped the lead onto his dog, which had just done its business against my hedge. He drew the animal towards him protectively, shaking his head. I saw his index finger twitching towards his temple, but he managed to scratch his ear instead.

'Well, I must be off,' he said. 'I'll leave you to your snails.'

He turned and set off at a brisk pace. I watched him until he was out of sight round the bend in the road. Such a nice person – he really had been hanging in there, trying to understand. A pity I couldn't enlighten him. But it was so difficult to go into explanations, especially in the cold and dark, and when it was bucketing down with rain and I was trying to save my snails from being splatted under heavy boots. Besides, what if he had children, and happened to mention that there were marked snails merrily sliming about in the vicinity? Word could get round, starting a snail hunt among neighbouring children, who might not observe all the finer points of the experimental process – such as *not* picking subjects up and carrying them off somewhere else.

I turned back to the task in hand. Anxiously, I searched the pavement for corpses. Luckily, that crunch I heard was only the scrape of a pebble against the concrete. I checked, yet again, for mollusc bodies that might have been squashed by cars or dog walkers. The snails were still all over the road. They hardly seemed to be moving at all. I stared at them for a while, puzzled. Surely they should be going somewhere? I crouched down and observed the one nearest to me. Its body was stretched out to its fullest extent in a shallow puddle, with its fat, fleshy foot spread out sideways. It looked as if it was luxuriating in a jacuzzi. In fact, all the puddles on the Tarmac were like a series of jacuzzis, each of them filled with snails enjoying their own private health spa.

I realised what the snails were up to. A long period of hot, dry weather had caused the snails' mucus to dry out, and they had been suffering badly in recent weeks. They were in need of moisture to absorb into their skins and replenish their mucus. Without this slime, movement was impossible. I knew that snails needed moisture for every single one of their functions: reproduction, growth and – particularly now – feeding. This rain marked the end of a particularly dry spell. They had been hunkering down in their shells, aestivating. By now, they must be starving. Soaking in puddles was the best and quickest way to replenish the vital ingredient that would switch on their feeding reflex and get their digestive juices flowing again. That was why they were not going anywhere. They had been enticed out of their rocky holes towards a place where they could be sure of a good soak.

I glanced round. All these snails, and not one single one of them mine or Sue's. I should have thought that, between us, we would have found at least a few. Scientists had a hard time, I was beginning to realise. Daily, they faced setbacks, such as not having the right equipment, not being able to obtain funding, the frustrations of getting their data in a tangle, disappointment when their results did not match their hypotheses.

For months now, I had enjoyed following the progress of my three fellow amateur scientists. I wondered if they ever felt as stuck as I did now. Nina was fascinated by the different ways in which people portrayed themselves on Facebook, and wondered what social or psychological factors influenced their profile pictures. Sam was having a whale of a time going to gigs – all in the cause of science, naturally. He wanted to test the theory that the crush at these events was not, as might be expected, at the front, but three rows back. To do this he was using a special pressure suit that had recently been developed for investigating crowd pressures. John was researching noctilucent clouds. These curious phenomena occur way up in the mesosphere, eighty kilometres high. The photos he posted were stunning, but to take them, and to do his research, John had to sacrifice his sleep for the entire summer, as the clouds could be seen only between midnight and pre-dawn.

Nevertheless, I envied John just now. While he was turning his gaze skywards, here was I, in a downpour at midnight, my eyes glued to the Tarmac, with nothing to show for it. What a sad contrast.

I found myself spending more and more time on Facebook, not just writing up my notes and following the other experiments, but also chuckling over the homing tales that poured in from gardeners. Most had, at one time or another, shared my frustrations, while pondering the question of homing instinct. Adding to our growing body of anecdotal evidence, many people contributed their own homing stories, some well within the bounds of possibility, others quite improbable – the snail equivalent of the big fish story.

Duncan posted that he was inundated with snails. He kept moving them to the field at the back of a car park, but within a day or two they were back. He wondered whether they were the same ones. So he selected ten, and numbered them 0 to 9. They all came back several times and it usually took them about two days. He reckoned that the distance travelled was twenty-five metres from the back of the house. In response to this, Kate said that she had done a similar experiment, ages ago, in her Australian garden, after becoming convinced that she was releasing the same snails time and time again. She painted the shells with cherry-red polish, and popped them by the creek behind her home to see if her suspicions were correct. She reported that some did indeed make it back.

Joy's snails were jet-propelled. Their trails of mucus actually began six feet above ground, up a wall, and disappeared under her weatherboarding. She speculated that they were addicted to the fibreglass insulation in her attic. She also reported that, somehow, the wily creatures had slimed their way into her plastic storage shed to eat wallpaper and boxes, and, with their tongues, they had scraped the pictures off the surfaces of some table mats.

Graham was a painter. In the 1980s and 1990s, he worked daily in his garden shed. On wet days, he habitually tossed snails over the garden wall into the overgrown back alley. Convinced that the size of the snail population remained exactly the same nevertheless, he put blobs of acrylic paint on their shells to see if they would come back. Several did, and were rewarded with a blob in another colour. Back into the alley they went. Some returned four or five times.

Some creatures homed unerringly to a very specific area. Two years earlier, Barrie had numbered the snails on his patio from 1 to 20, using white marking fluid, and taken them off to areas of waste ground, sometimes fifty metres away, other times seventy, but always on rocky terrain. He found that fifty per cent of the total would return to exactly the same spot. Half of those ended up on one side of the patio doors, half on the other, each returning without fail to the same side they were collected from.

Even more determined not to be ousted from their homes were the Olympic-standard molluscs belonging to John. He took lots of snails from his back garden through his terraced house and released them at the front. He reported: 'They all headed straight up the front wall with the clear aim of going straight back over the roof to where they came from.'

Jason's snails far exceeded established speed records. Having numbered them, he placed ten of these athletes in different locations near his terraced house, including the front garden and the garden of his next-door neighbour. The results were startling. Snail number one was home within twenty-four hours; snail number two travelled over two walls, across one garden and round (or over) a shed the size of a garage. Jason added that the snail was now 'resting next to the growing sunflower'. He did not say how long this journey took, but as the crow flies, it was a distance of about thirty metres.

Many enthusiasts found inventive ways to keep track of their snails. Celine, from France, tied sewing thread to their shells. As the creatures crept along, the thread unwound itself slowly from a cotton reel attached to a fixed point. She started them off from the wall of her house, and found that, after going wandering overnight, they returned, following the wall, over distances of up to thirty metres.

There were also letters that came by snail mail. One was sent to me via the BBC. A lady from Scotland asked if I could solve a particular problem. Every morning, she would find droves of snails sliming up her front door, and every morning she would remove them. But by the evening they were back again, beginning their ascent all over again. The clue to this compulsive climbing lay, she guessed, in the fact that it was a wooden door. All her neighbours had white uPVC doors, and none of them had ever seen these mountaineering molluscs. This seemed simple enough: surely, the snails just preferred wooden doors. But the lady wanted to know why, and so did I. Was it the varnish that appealed to their taste buds? Was its surface warmer than the surrounding surfaces, helping these cold-blooded creatures to keep warm? Maybe it was east-facing, and the snails crawled up the door every evening in preparation for an early-morning sunbath. Perhaps it was a very old door, with notches and crevices for hiding in. Or maybe it was new, and had that delicious smell of new wood that sent the creatures into an olfactory frenzy.

One thing was clear – this was a subject for yet another experiment that I would never have time to do. I was now seeing experiments everywhere I looked, and they all involved those compelling things that I had never considered before – those maddening variables. There is no convert like a new convert. I was beginning to think like a scientist, but I lacked the essential infrastructure of knowledge that would allow me to carry through all the myriad research ideas that flooded my brain.

My inadequacies really hit home when David Dunstan, Professor of Experimental Physics at Queen Mary College, University of London, contacted me. He told me about an extraordinary experiment that he had carried out over a six-month period in 2001. His research paper was entitled 'The homing instinct of garden snails: Drift or diffusion?'. In a small garden, he had searched for snails. Every time he found one, he dabbed it with white marking fluid, and threw it over a brick wall and Tarmac footpath into wasteland. 'Snails that returned and were found again were given an extra mark each time they were found. In total, snails were found, marked and thrown over the wall 1,395 times. Because many snails returned, the total number of distinct snails observed was much less, only 416.'

All the returns were plotted on a graph showing the cumulative fraction of snails that were found after one return, two returns and so on, up to twelve returns. Professor Dunstan could find no evidence of homing instinct. He concluded that their behaviour was stochastic. So now I had a new term to engage with. 'Stochastic' means random diffusion, by which the snails, after wandering round aimlessly, somehow manage to end up at home. This is different to what he termed 'drift', meaning under the influence of homing instinct.

He concluded that there was no good reason for gardeners to kill snails, because: 'Killing snails is futile, for those found and killed are only a small sample of a much larger population, and on our data it takes months to reduce the total population significantly. Most plants need protection for a few weeks early in the growing season, and for that, it is sufficient to remove the snails from the garden.' Obviously, he hadn't come across snails like mine, which rampage throughout the summer, but on the subject of removal, at least, we were both agreed.

I was bowled over by this piece of research, even though it contradicted our findings completely. I put him in touch with Dave, who agreed to look at his study – particularly at the fearsomely intricate and complicated graph that demonstrated his results. I was delighted (but slightly nervous), when, as a result of this, he was invited to the BBC studios to present his research at a recording of *Material World*. Dave and I also gave an update of our own findings – which made for a lively discussion.

After the recording, I asked Professor Dunstan about his experiment. We sat on the steps of the church outside Broadcasting House for nearly an hour, while he patiently explained that awesome graph with all its mathematical symbols. It is a testament to his teaching ability that he managed to teleport himself down from university-level physics to my own level of understanding, offering flashes of illumination like sunshine bursting through gaps in the cloud. I couldn't decide what was most impressive: Professor Dunstan's tenacity in chucking snails 1,395 times, or the sheer bloody-mindedness of all those creatures that made it back over the wall many times over.

I found it interesting rather than worrying that we had reached entirely different conclusions about snail homing. After all, this was the stuff of science and it made for stimulating debate. In the past, I had always imagined science to be a steady progression, whereby brilliant minds carried forward the research of previous brilliant minds, leading to mind-boggling discoveries and truths about the universe that were now so well-established that they seemed to be set in stone. Now, I realised that it wasn't so clear cut. Maybe there were black holes into which our knowledge could suddenly disappear, like our ancestors' conviction that the Earth was flat. (Wow, I thought, some day far into the future, someone might even find a particle that travels faster than the speed of light!)

Professor Dunstan's research reminded me of my interest in the effect of repeated disturbance on snails' behaviour. I was particularly captivated by the idea that snails had a memory, and that this was connected to a strong sense of smell. I was inspired to carry out my own, ad hoc experiments. If I removed them from their favourite nosh, would the memory of its delicious aroma guide them back home?

Late one afternoon, I hunted round the garden for any snail that had been part of previous experiments. I soon found some maroon-spots snoozing in their usual day-lily patch, and took these down to the rockery by the silver birch tree. The yellow-spots still rested by day in the sisyrinchium, but at night they crept stealthily over a short stretch of lawn and feasted on my strawberries. I managed to catch some of them in the act, and transported them round the side of the house to the front garden. I deposited them in a patch of wild geraniums and ferns. Their new menu was limited, and probably not at all to their taste, but it was cool and damp in their new location; at least they would have a comfortable night while deciding whether or not to embark on the long slime home. This would necessitate a long trek along the concrete path in front of the house, and an even longer slog round the side, until they were at last back in the strawberry patch. There was little or no vegetation at all along the way – just a few weeds

growing in the cracks of the concrete and along the neighbour's fence. I felt a bit bad about this. Would the challenge
be too much for them?

After this, I wandered round the garden, suddenly aware
of how much needed doing. It was now mid-July, and still
very hot and dry. Because of the experiments, all maintenance and tidying up, pruning and trimming had taken a
back seat in my priorities. Dandelions and grass forced their
way through cracks in the paving stones of the patio. Tall
tomato stems bent at crazy angles over a bed of spinach and
Swiss chard – when they were all tiny seedlings, it had for
some reason seemed a good idea to plant them together.
Now the tomatoes needed supporting; the green fruits were
rotting in the ground. A row of raspberry canes against the
fence had escaped from under their restraining wires. They
leaned dizzily outwards towards the adjacent lawn, as if
searching for their offspring – baby raspberry canes that
were springing up everywhere. The grass surrounding
them had grown so high that I hadn't noticed them before.

A passion flower, which for many years mushroomed
prodigiously over a trellised arch, had given up the ghost.
Only its thin, leafless branches remained, still intertwined
round the wire squares of the trellis. Normally I would have
cut it down and replaced it with a new climber, but now I
saw beauty in those twisted, skeletal limbs. Here was
Nature's sculpture – a tribute to a life well-lived and a
reminder that all things have their time. In pots and flower
beds, the tall spikes of purple toadflax had seeded themselves,
spreading everywhere. In previous years, they would have
been severely trimmed, corralled into tidy clumps. But I

could see how the bees loved them, buzzing in eager droves about their deep lilac petals. The toadflax would have to stay until the flowers faded and died.

The garden was busy doing its own thing, without my intervention. Even now, it offered up its gifts – but on its own terms. Clumps of hardy perennials formed islands of colour among the weeds. On the apple trees, unripened Russets and Coxes had begun to weigh down the branches; against the warm, south-facing wall of the house, the bright-green beads of miniature grapes peeped between leaves on the vine. The garden was a mess, but there was a wholesome naturalness to it that was unexpectedly pleasing. Balanced between total neglect and superimposed order, it had settled itself into a homely, cottagey, semi-wilderness.

I burrowed about under the silver birch, still hunting for snails from previous experiments. Here grew cranesbills and plantains, ferns and yellow archangel, and the tiny, blue-petalled speedwell that crept all over my lawn. Other creatures were about, too, hiding round the tree and in the leaf mould below it – creatures that so far I had managed never to notice. I could just, with my naked eye, make out the larvae of a beetle. I found tiny grubs and centipedes. Under a piece of wood, a ghostly, almost transparent white spider with very long legs had wrapped itself in a cocoon of fleece. Was it an embryo? There were microscopic black dots in the fleece; were they eggs, or just specks of dirt? I had no idea, and for the first time it mattered to me that that I did not know.

A butterfly was sunning itself against my house wall, beating its wings repeatedly against the warm concrete surface. As I crouched down to look, it fluttered away. The sun warmed my back, and it felt good. A delicious lightness began to suffuse my whole body, starting with a tingling in my toes and spreading upwards until it ended in a deep, contented sigh. Everything felt good in this garden.

SEVENTEEN

The Final Reckoning

nce, on a still evening, I went out to water my ever-diminishing hostas. As I approached the pot, I heard a faint, rasping sound. I could actually hear the snails demolishing the leaves of the plant. Looking closely, I could see square patches where their tongues had been at work. The creatures' efficiency was awesome: they were eating machines. During their gastronomic frenzy, while their tongues were scraping the best bits away from my hostas, their salivary glands would be secreting mucus and enzymes to aid their digestion.

Earlier that day, I had squashed a snail by mistake, possibly injuring its internal organs. Hastily, I took it to the furthest end of the garden, hoping that the snail might repair itself against the odds. For a day or two it languished in its pitiful state, then it disappeared. But the incident prompted me to do some research on snails' innards: what happened inside a body that ate several times its own weight every day?

When I was a fifteen-year-old, studying for my O levels, biology was one of my favourite subjects. Our teacher was an ex-GP, who had the knack of bringing our lessons alive, particularly when describing the human digestive system.

We had to draw a diagram for homework. I remember carefully labelling the different parts, starting at the top – mouth, teeth and tongue – all the way down to the bottom. In those days, bottoms were still the subject of mild embarrassment, and the word 'anus' was never mentioned. As for human reproduction, that had not yet reached the biology syllabus. We were still stuck firmly in the realms of the amoeba, or, if we were lucky, the rabbit. Digestion was a joy. It was a relief at last to get to grips with a topic so real and so functional.

The large intestine was a revelation to me. All those yards and yards of pipework. Yet the stomach was just a small pouch. With our healthy adolescent appetites, we could scarcely comprehend how the copious contents of our lunch boxes would ever fit inside. Somewhere, hiding beneath the folds of our skin, more body parts were silently beavering away, doing their thing: mouth and tongue, salivary glands, oesophagus, stomach with its digestive glands, pancreas, liver, small and large intestines, anus. All our meals moving downwards in an orderly progression, over and over again.

I had always imagined that my garden snails would have a far simpler arrangement. Inside that shell there would be nothing but an enormous stomach, and not much else. It never occurred to me that snails, too, could have a complicated digestive system. When, as an amateur scientist, I finally got my head round all its convolutions, I was astonished to learn that it was just as complex as my own.

Most of the intestine, together with the heart, liver and other body organs, are referred to collectively as the visceral mass. They are located in the trunk of the snail, contained in a bag called the visceral sac. The intestine itself is so long that it often exceeds the length of the foot. If this long tube were coiled flat like a pinwheel, the animal would have to stretch out to at least twice its width to accommodate it. Instead, the visceral mass, as it develops, coils into a spiral that becomes bunched up under the shell – the shell takes its own spiral

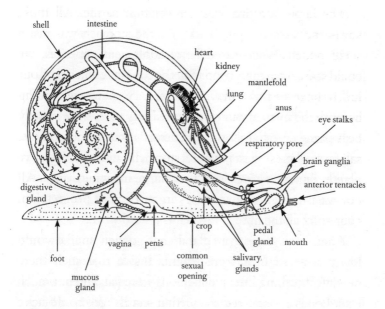

The snail's anatomy.

shape to fit the form of this hump, not the other way round, its main function being to protect these internal organs. Everything spins round while the snail is still in the egg, so that the opening of the anus is situated almost above the mouth, seemingly a most unsavoury arrangement.

The snail's mouth is often difficult to see, a mere slit underneath its front part. It leads into a cave-like opening called the buccal cavity, in the roof of which is a small fixed jaw. The floor is occupied by the buccal mass, a hefty combination of cartilage and muscle, which operates the tongue – the radula. But this formidable organ is nothing like any normal tongue. It is a fearsome and wondrous piece of equipment, looking like a narrow rasp, made up of thousands of minute and very sharp teeth arranged in many rows. When teeth become damaged or worn, the snail can manufacture new ones.

For my semi-decimated hostas, the next stage of the journey, via a narrow oesophagus, is the crop, an elongated, oval-shaped sac that contains the salivary glands, which aid digestion. They then wind their way along an intestine, which leads to the digestive gland at the snail's posterior end. This organ, the largest in the visceral mass, has three purposes: it secretes digestive juices into the crop, it stores nutrients, and it converts these nutrients into energy to fuel its own activity – digesting all the fibre in my plants is hard work.

When the digestive gland has done its job, my now-massacred hostas are squeezed into a long, looped intestine, finishing their journey at the anus above the snail's head. Poo is evacuated at frequent intervals, green or black, depending on the snail's recent diet.

The snail's 'brain' is also in its head: a bunch of nerve cells called the cerebral ganglia. This has been termed a 'scatterbrain', because the ganglia separately control all the different bodily systems. How fitting it seems that these ganglia are so near the mouth and common sexual opening. It is like a one-track brain, reflecting the priorities of a creature that spends almost all of its waking life eating or mating.

The internal workings of my snails were gruesomely illustrated when, following up the experiment I had done a couple of weeks earlier, I discovered the location of one of my displaced yellow-spotted snails. These were the hapless creatures that I had plucked from their paradise in the strawberry patch in the back garden and transported to the wilderness of the front. I'd hoped to find out how snails would react to being displaced from their favourite feeding sites and, most significantly, whether memory (possibly linked to smell) was a factor in their subsequent behaviour.

Firmly stuck to the rough-cast concrete of the side wall of the house, a few centimetres above the concrete path, my courageous snail had battled its way, in the heat, all the way from the furthest point in the front garden, slimed round the corner of the house, and staggered a further ten metres, before throwing in the towel. Why had it climbed the wall? Perhaps it felt less vulnerable to predators; maybe it was trying to top up its essential reserves of lime.

I have to confess that I had, in fact, noticed it a couple of days before, in exactly the same position. I'd assumed – hopefully or naively – that it was having a rest. When I prised it away from its horrible grave, it barely weighed a thing. Peering into its shell, I could see, deep inside, a hard, gluey, grey lump. It had shrunk to virtually nothing. Mollusc flesh is made up mostly of water; the snail had, in effect, evaporated in the heat. Full of remorse, I buried it, with full honours, in the strawberry patch where it belonged.

The only positive outcome of this sorry tale was that, if I had needed extra proof of a snail's homing instinct, this was it. It also suggested that senses were a factor. Did olfactory memory play a part in its heroic attempt to reach the back garden? Could the recollection of that tantalising straw-berry aroma have guided it towards home?

There was no other possible motive for it to use up its precious mucus by sliming along two concrete paths, a total distance of thirty metres, in the burning heat, unless it had a purpose. My snail was desperate to get back to those succulent strawberries. If, while in exile, it had simply been feeling a bit peckish, or in need of a mate, then all it had to do was make a short trip over to the rockery, where it would have found dozens of cousins happily feasting on my rock plants. Here, to my mind, was strong evidence to support both homing instinct and the existence of memory. From the front garden, the snail would not have been able to smell the strawberries, yet it must have had some recollection of that scent and where it was located. But I had no proof, other than my own eyes, and a photo I took on the spot. Doubters could easily accuse me of 'planting' my snail. However, I swear that everything I have just written is the truth, the whole truth, and nothing but the truth.

Fortunately, new results were coming in. These were the findings from the online Great Snail Swap. Those taking part had reported returns from between ten metres and thirty metres, with one intrepid creature managing an impressive one-hundred-metre hike through a wood. These results all supported the homing theory. Yet it was disappointing that, in the end, only about thirty people had bothered to take part in this unique, national experiment. Maybe the cause was people's lack of time, or their being away on holiday. Perhaps, during the extremely hot spell, they were unable to find any snails. Could the lack of response simply be put down to British reserve? Borrowing a strimmer or chatting over the garden fence on a Sunday afternoon is within the bounds of neighbourly sociability, but swapping snails instead of tools is going too far.

At least St John's school's pilot experiment was a success. During the summer, the children, teachers and parents had all been out and about snail spotting. Several pupils reported the safe return of snails, a few apparently homing, as the crow flies, over distances of up to half a mile. Whether these determined creatures took a short cut across gardens, or slogged up the main road, no one will ever know. One was spotted beside a Spar shop very close to the school; another was discovered just about to cross the bridge into town. A few disorientated molluscs were seen wandering about outside the school gates. All sightings were dutifully plotted on the class map by the children, who noted their date of return and the position in relation to their homes.

One might question the scientific reliability of these eight- and nine-year-old children. Their results will never get to the peer-review stage or be reported in *Nature*. But their experience went far beyond an enjoyable science project. Not only had it brought a classroom subject alive, but it had opened their eyes to the infinite wonder of the natural world around them.

The final of 'So You Want to be a Scientist?' was drawing near. It would take place at Aston University, Birmingham, as part of the British Science Festival. Michelle emailed me to ask for a summary of our research to present to the judges, who would also be reading through all my notes. The judges were the clinical psychologist, author and broadcaster Professor Tanya Byron; the science editor of *The Times*, Mark Henderson; and acoustic engineer Professor Trevor Cox.

Presenting my work to such people, all experts in their field, was a daunting prospect. My summary had to be good. No waffling or going off into flights of fancy, or dreaming up a zillion other ideas for investigating snail behaviour. The judges wanted to know exactly what we had found out about snail homing, and they wanted hard evidence – all squeezed into one page of A4. After much head-scratching, I wrote:

Results from Research into Homing Distance of Cornu aspersum *(garden snail):*

There is much anecdotal evidence that, like the homing pigeons, snails are able to find their way back to their own gardens, if ejected. Distances of up to a mile or even more have been reported. Yet this had not been substantiated with scientific evidence. So I wanted to find out for myself if these accounts of epic journeys by snails were true, or not. But before establishing distance, *it was necessary to find out whether snails actually had a homing* instinct.

To begin, I set up two pilot experiments in my own garden. For each experiment, I collected separate samples of snails from two different areas of my garden. I called these areas 'Home' and 'Away' bases. The snails were marked, counted and numbered. The distance between the bases was measured. They were then released midway in a neutral – i.e. unattractive to Cornu aspersum *– space. The release point was the centre of a tin tray on which a compass circle had been drawn, with the compass points marked. As the snails left the circle, their exit points were marked, and recorded, to establish their direction of travel. The snails were monitored over several weeks to check their progress.*

The results from these two experiments showed startling evidence of homing instinct over 8 metres and 10 metres, with Fisher's exact test showing probability values of 0.0014 and 0.00004 respectively. Two more instinct experiments were carried out on the university campus by Dave Hodgson. Again, the results showed powerful evidence of homing instinct.

The next step was to establish distance. *A national experiment was set up online: The Great Snail Swap. Neighbours collected snails from a particular patch in their gardens, marked and counted them, and swapped them over. On the online questionnaire, they recorded when the first snail arrived back, and also the distance (divided into 'bands') between the two bases. Also recorded were barriers and weather.*

Results:

Findings in this experiment were complicated by a spell of exceptionally dry weather, during which many snails disappeared – presumably into shade, sealed up in their epiphragms. But in those instances where snails were recovered over short distances, between 10 and 30 metres, there was strong evidence of homing instinct. Over longer distances, results were inconclusive. This could have been due to the many variables, e.g. a wood; a type of barrier, e.g. road or building; the hot weather; or the actual distance itself.

Conclusions:

From the evidence so far, it seems clear that Cornu aspersum *does have a homing instinct, and can 'home' to distances between 10 and 30 metres. Beyond this, conclusions are difficult due to the variables mentioned above. But implications for frustrated gardeners, who want to know exactly how far away they can take their garden snails, are that, on the evidence so far, it would be safe to take and place them elsewhere at a distance of say, 100 to 200 metres. Therefore, there is no need to kill them. The implications of not using pesticides are: healthier*

microorganisms in the soil, and less danger of poisoning to
pets and birds. And the feel-good factor for humans!

For distances of over 30 metres, I would like to devise
further experiments in more controlled conditions, working
with only one variable at a time. Although not replicating
natural conditions, it would hopefully move us forward in
our quest to find out exactly how far we must take our
snails before they come back to chomp on our precious
lettuces. It would also provide valuable information on
snails' behaviour, such as adaptation to disturbance and
to different conditions, and also how snails remember their
journeys! I would like to do much more research on homing
and behaviour, and memory.

To accompany this report, Dave had designed a beautiful poster, which would form the basis of my PowerPoint presentation. This set out our objectives, how the experiment was designed, our results, and our conclusions. To make my life easier, he had also incorporated the data sets from four of our homing instinct experiments, showing the statistical analysis using Fisher's exact test, which measured the probability, or non-probability, of a certain event happening.

After I had finished my report, I read it through several times, frowning. Something was missing. Not the science: I had, I thought, adequately explained our research. I had even mentioned the dreaded Fisher's test. It also felt good that I would have a definite structure for my talk. I felt confident about presenting a convincing case, especially because Dave, too, would have his slot, giving his take on the summer's research.

The results of his experiments on the Cornwall Campus were just as impressive as my own. In the first one, over a distance of thirty metres, eight out of fifty-four Home snails had returned to Home base with no crossovers, and seven out of seventy-four Away snails to Away base, with just one crossover (Fisher's exact test: 0.00014). In the second, over eight metres, twenty out of eighty-one Home snails had returned home, while twenty out of sixty-eight Away snails had slogged it back to base, with a few awkward customers from either side doing a crossover. At first glance, going simply by the proportion of returns, these results did not seem spectacular, but statistically, they were very significant, giving strong support to the homing theory: Fisher's exact test revealed the probability of this occurring by chance as being 0.00001. To me, those five noughts were mind-boggling.

But there was still a problem. The length of the talk would be limited to just five minutes, as all four finalists were to be recorded for the next *Material World* programme. This should have been a relief – less time to waffle on about my other experiments. But when listening to previous BBC recordings, in which I had been explaining the project, I had been struck by how slowly I spoke. My long-drawn-out vowels sent me to sleep, and would probably have the same effect on the audience. Speed was paramount if I wanted to squeeze several months' research into such a short space of time.

It was then that I realised what was niggling me most of all. In that vital five minutes, I wanted to be able to encapsulate the *essence* of my research. The summer had not just been about play: it had evoked something that I felt deep inside. I had started the project solely in the spirit of scientific enquiry, hoping to have some fun along the way. At first, in the excitement of doing the experiments, any ethical and moral questions were little more than vague musings sitting uneasily at the back of my mind. But these gentle stirrings had gathered pace and energy, finally spinning my brain into a whirlwind. Something profound had been kindled deep within me, and I longed to express it.

I felt as if my discoveries held a truth. I wanted to tell the world that this research was not just about the homing instinct of snails. The implications were far, far wider. They were about my relationship with my fellow creatures and how I could live lightly on the planet without harming them. My snails were but the catalysts in my conversion. They had aroused deep thoughts within me, revealing themselves as unlikely symbols for sustainability.

If I poisoned a snail with pellets, this would affect not only its digestion, but also its heart, lung and brain – its whole being. The systems of the Earth – biological, chemical, physical – are a macro-reflection of the internal systems of my snails. They are all connected. We disturb a single one at our peril: the whole fragile structure would begin to wobble round the edges.

Now, I was absolutely convinced that I needed to rethink my relationship with other creatures. I had examined my attitude to the inconvenient pests that somehow got in my way. Not just the snails that spoilt my garden, but the moths on my fruit trees, the mice in the larder, the ants crawling over the kitchen worktops. Where should I draw the line, and decide to save one animal but kill another? What would be the consequences for my own well-being if my emotional skin thickened and I became inured to the suffering of other creatures? I certainly had no definitive answers, but the question was affecting me deeply.

During the last few years I had been on a journey of conscience. Over this summer, my thoughts had crystallised, my world view altered so sharply that all doubts had dissolved. If I found a row of eaten cabbages, this did not justify mollusc death. Only my cabbages were in danger, not my life – or even my supper. Seeing the mangled leaves made me want to scream. But this did not merit a death sentence for creatures that were only trying to survive. Particularly when there was an alternative, a kinder way to protect our gardens and our crops: I simply had to remove my snails from my plants.

Perhaps we could think more laterally about solutions and invent more creative ways of halting munching molluscs in their tracks: trapping them in a gooey but harmless polymer gel, for example, or how about fitting a tiny but powerful magnet to their shells? The snails might leave my garden en masse, propelled inexorably towards the North Pole. Out of the craziest ideas, who knows what useful research might develop?

I knew that the judges would understand the implications of the research. There was no need to hammer the point home. Yet I longed to end my talk with a rallying cry: 'If our results save the life of one single snail, the project will not have been in vain!' But even I could hear how squirmingly melodramatic this sounded. I could already imagine the hatchet faces of the more cynical members of the audience.

All I could do was present our findings, unemotionally and factually. In the end, people always make up their own minds.

Three days after receiving the award, I stepped out into the mellow September sunshine, relishing the silence and the cool air on my arms. In the far corner of the garden, a breeze rustled the delicate branches of the silver birch. Swirling round its papery trunk, they dipped and swayed and danced in perpetual motion. The tree seemed to be chuckling to itself.

The past few days had passed in a blur of bemusement and wonder. I had not expected to win. I'd started the project with a simple question, letting the excitement of finding things out sweep me along from one day to the next. It had been a summer of joy, in which my long-frozen brain was at last beginning to thaw out. Now, having won, I was proud of what Dave and I had achieved.

I was back with my snails, which were at this moment creeping out of their holes. I could see their lower tentacles waving about, sniffing out their evening meals. Finding them was easy. I simply followed their slime trails to some flowerpots at the base of the trellis, still interwoven with the dead limbs of the passion flower. Close to its knotted base, in a last desperate bid for life, this plant had put forth new shoots. The young tendrils had just started to latch on to a wooden support. My exploring fingers disturbed some dozy woodlice, snoozing under a rotten plank. They always seemed to alternate their lives of bone idleness with bouts of frantic activity. I watched them for a minute, wondering how they managed to scurry about so quickly on their minuscule legs.

I went round to the front and poked about in the rockery. The project might officially have come to an end, but I was still curious to know what had become of all the snails that had helped me with my experiments. A couple more had returned from one of the instinct experiments, and were hiding under a boulder next to a sleeping toad. The toad woke up, and froze, its flanks pulsating rapidly with each breath. I quickly replaced its cover. In the spring, this engaging creature would be back in my pond, producing its next generation. I wondered why it never ate any of the slugs and snails. According to all the organic gardening experts, this was the main purpose of introducing toads and frogs. But, in my garden, the mollusc population never diminished – toads, slugs and snails all happily co-existed.

The pond, neglected for weeks, was smothered with weed. I scooped up handfuls of the slimy blanket. Now I could see the pond skaters as they skimmed along the surface of the water. In its depths, newts darted between the long stems of lilies. A dragonfly with pale blue wings and a very long body whizzed past my ear, did a circuit of the pond and settled on some tall rushes. I moved closer, holding my breath. The dragonfly was not at all perturbed by my presence, allowing me to admire the delicate pattern on its quivering wings. Then, something else caught my eye. At the other side of the pond, on the wooden trellis separating my garden from the carport, three spiders had spun webs inside three adjacent diamonds – a terrace of shimmering new homes. It was extraordinary to see how the spiders had found just the right twig or strut on which to hook the outer threads, and how geometrically perfect the patterns were. In the centre of each web sat its proud owner, waiting to ensnare its next meal. For a while I stood still, and marvelled.

It was time for my own tea. By the back door, a group of hungry snails had selected their dish of the day. They were attacking the lettuce seedlings that I had planted a few days earlier, hoping for a late crop. Carefully, I prised the thieving molluscs away from the leaves and carried them away to the end of the garden, knowing that they would be back in a day or two. Sometime soon, I needed to find a way of keeping them contained until I could march them over to the woodland. I watched them curl up sulkily inside their shells.

All was as it was supposed to be. Tiny shivers tingled up and down my spine, bubbling up from a well of contentment deep inside me. In the garden, nothing had changed – except me.

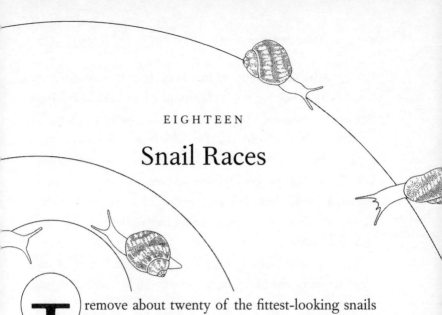

EIGHTEEN

Snail Races

I remove about twenty of the fittest-looking snails from my terrarium – the holding bay that I use while storing up enough of them to make a trip to the woodland worthwhile. This is no detention centre for illegal aliens facing deportation. It is more like a luxury hotel. On top of a gravel base covered with pebbles, earth and moss, there are flowerpots, bits of wood, a saucer of water and the snail version of a full English breakfast – the pathetic remains of the lupins and delphiniums that they'd already chomped before I detained them at my pleasure.

I place the twenty athletes in a row, seeing which ones scoot off fastest towards some strategically positioned petunia petals. Those that faff about or go to sleep are disqualified and popped straight back in the terrarium. Ten hopefuls are selected, and placed in a plastic container with some moss and damp stones, with French beans for snacking on.

Now, they're travelling with me on a train, discreetly out of sight in my holdall. I'm on my way to the World Snail

Racing Championships, held every July at Congham in Norfolk. I'm hoping that at least one of my snails will beat the time established in 1995 by Archie, who entered the *Guinness Book of Records* for the fastest dash across a thirteen-inch course. Two of my champions, still dotted with Desire, have come from last year's instinct experiments. I found them hanging out in their original resting places, and I reckoned this demonstrated their tenacity and survival instinct.

I gaze out of the window, watching huge, flat fields roll by, rows and rows of cabbages or leeks or broccoli growing in the black earth. So much expanse, so different from my part of Devon. Where I live, the clouds nudge the hills from above, gently caressing their curves. Here, a vast sky and looming clouds swoop down upon the flat countryside. I feel as if I am swimming in an upside-down, infinite sea.

I love train journeys. It is so good to get away from the everyday chores and petty irritations that build up when I spend too much time in the house. Sitting here just now is an enforced relaxation. It gives me time to reflect on all the snail-related happenings of the past year. There has been an exciting update to the experiments on the Cornwall Campus – those carried out under Dave's supervision by his third-year student, Sarah. In the year since the *Material World* broadcast, many of their Home and Away snails have been sliming back to their respective bases – a wall and a pond thirty metres apart – and have settled back again. The research continues; in fact, it has reached a whole new level. Dave is now planning further distance experiments for the autumn. This time, the snails will be tagged with wafer-thin copper plates fixed to their shells. Then they'll be tracked with a metal detector, saving hours and hours of searching.

In my own garden, I've been making similar discoveries, finding both yellow- and maroon-spots from my first two experiments snoozing in the day lilies and the sisyrinchium. During the past year, they must have gone on some long-haul journeys round the garden: certainly, they haven't been there the whole time. The dogged tenacity of these creatures in their homing habits never fails to amaze me. They simply refuse to give up. Could there be a lesson here for us?

Last month, Dave and I presented the project at the Cheltenham Science Festival, where I also had the honour of being one of a panel of speakers at an event called 'How Does Your Garden Grow?'. The most rewarding experience of the Festival for me took place in the BBC education tent, where Michelle had organised a homing instinct experiment, mainly for children. Dave and I, together with some young-sters, searched in the nearby park for some snails, and brought them to the tent. They were marked and given names, then released in an adapted version of our experi-ments. Snail races and some entertaining snail-based education proved popular with both the kids and their parents. I was surprised how many adults were wary of, even disgusted by, snails. A particular triumph that afternoon was persuading one reluctant lady to place a snail on the back of her hand. She told me it was one of the bravest things she had done in her life.

I spent five days at the Festival, instead of the two days I had originally planned for my own events. Looking through the programme, I became greedier and greedier. I wanted to go to all the talks, every single event, and join in all the fun and games. In the space of one year, I have morphed into a science junkie. My stay ended, literally, with a bang, watching a children's demonstration by Professor Robert Winston of spectacular and wacky experiments.

For years, I've bought science magazines and followed more and more science programmes on the radio. On winning the award I was offered the opportunity to write an article about my snail-homing research for the magazine *Mollusc World*. Since then, I've extended my range of interests, my brain hoovering up any fascinating snippet of scientific information. From cosmology to stem cells, alpha rhythms to patterns in nature, a new world of exciting knowledge has opened up to me. I've joined the Conchological Society of Great Britain and Ireland.

Last October, I went to my first Conchological Society meeting at the Natural History Museum in London. The members were very welcoming, making allowances for my beginner status – even though they could rattle off the Latin names of different species and body parts as if they were items on a shopping list. All are experts in their own speciality; most have studied zoology or related subjects to a high level. I could see that I was on a rapid learning curve here, and resolved to widen my scope far beyond the study of homing behaviour.

I can understand why conchology is such an absorbing interest. All those strikingly different markings – speckles, stripes, dots and dashes – make shells a collector's dream. I had a small collection of seashells already. Recently, I've begun my own collection of snails' shells. Not knowing quite where to start, I decided to begin with something small. A member of the Conchological Society kindly sent me a sample of balea – tiny snails a few millimetres wide and little more than a centimetre long, with highly elongated coned shells that have a sharp point at the end. They are elephantine compared to some species of truncatellina, which are so minute (1.8–2mm by 0.9mm) that conchologists must go armed with sieves and magnifying glasses to search for them in their grassy or rocky habitats. Their distribution covers the south coast of England, including Devon. It would be exciting to find one so near my home, although with my dodgy sight I'll need a very powerful instrument.

At the other end of the scale, African land snails have shells more than twenty centimetres long. Now popular as pets in Britain, they do so much damage to crops in their native countries that they make my *Cornu aspersum* look positively saintly. A particularly odd shell is that of *Semilimax pyrenaicus*, which is found in the Pyrenees and in Ireland. *Semilimax* means 'half slug', and the cover that it carries on the lower half of its body is little more than an apology for a shell. This strange creature appears to be a snail that has decided it would get along better in life without a proper shell, but hasn't quite had the courage to cross over to full slughood. For protection, its shell would be as much use as a toy shield to a grown man. As the animal crawls along, it seems to be wearing a pair of very brief briefs.

Conchologists are still debating whether dead snail shells decay more quickly than living ones that have been exposed to the elements, and also whether dead shells survive longer on the surface of the soil than those buried within it. If the soil conditions are right – that is, with enough chalk – shells can be preserved for hundreds, even thousands of years. But even deep inside the soil, they can also be subject to chemical attack. To complicate matters further, bacteria deep within the earth can burrow into the grooves between the whorls of the shell and cause decay quite rapidly. And, as I have discovered, there is abrasion due to extreme heat – as well as cold.

I still haven't decided exactly how I'll collect my shells. One thing's for sure: they won't have a live inhabitant inside. The problem for collectors is that when snails die, the shells soon lose their colour, due to weathering from sun and rain. Eventually, when empty, they turn milky white. There is a way to collect fresh shells, but it is rather gruesome. First, the snail must be killed, either by plunging it in boiling water or, for larger species, winkling its body out of its house with a pin and discarding it. The shells are then dried thoroughly inside and out. Some keen and determined collectors do obtain shells by this method. For me, to kill a snail for its shell would be as heartless as catching a butterfly in a net and pinning it onto a board.

One phenomenon I've never got to the bottom of is the mysterious mass grave, with all its ghostly white shells, that I found in the rockery of my Surrey garden all those years ago. Since then, I have often encountered dead snails huddled together under boulders and in crevices, and I have not yet discovered the reason. Perhaps the elephants' graveyard theory is the nearest I will ever get: knowing that death is imminent, they lumber back to the burial places of their ancestors.

A back issue of *Mollusc World* is open on the table in front of me as the train speeds along. Absorbed in an article about the ways in which shells have been used round the world for personal adornment, I reach down absent-mindedly to fish my lunch box out of my holdall. As I place it on the table, there's a strangled shriek from mobile-phone lady opposite, who, for the past half-hour, has been engaged in a heated and very public split with her boyfriend. My lunch box is *not* my lunch box. My snails, fed up with their incarceration, have all slimed to the lid of their container and are stuck upside down near the air holes. An upside down snail attached to a transparent lid is not a pretty sight to anyone who is not fond of snails: the foot of the animal spreads out wide and the rippling effect of its muscles on the underside of its sole can, to the uninitiated, appear quite menacing. Even revolting, I think in amazement, as the young woman sweeps up her bag, coat and phone and disappears down the carriage. Still, now I have the table to myself.

I'm exploring Congham cricket field, waiting for the World Snail Racing Championships to begin. I'm enjoying the atmosphere of this village fete. Dotted round the field are the usual tried-and-trusted stalls – tombola, plants, hot dogs, second-hand books – and a band. For the past twenty-five years, it has been an annual event in aid of the local church. But at one o'clock, an hour before the fete is due to start, a deluge almost puts a stop to proceedings.

However, it is business as usual for the snails. They, at least, are in their element. And also undeterred by the weather, Liz and Neil Riseborough are setting up the course with their usual panache and good humour, as they have been doing for many years. Soon, in spite of the downpour, punters begin to gather round the table. Children, eagerly clutching snails, are pushed to the front of the crowd by proud parents. A cameraman and sound engineer from a television station try to protect their precious equipment under hoods and capes. It is hard to believe that this event can attract such wide media coverage. It must surely be the most laid-back competition on the planet.

For a start, there are hardly any rules. There are fifteen snails in each heat, and provided no one is left out, any number of snails belonging to a particular person can enter; so far, the rain has worked in most people's favour, as with fewer participants, more snails per owner can try their luck. The species of snail is supposed to be limited to the common garden snail, but a few cepaeas – small, but very nippy – have crept in somehow. Nor is there a minimum age, for snails or humans, so the speedier juveniles are much in evidence, deafeningly cheered on by their equally juvenile owners. The whole afternoon is a delight.

'Come on, Concho! Come on, Speckle, Bandy, Fibonacci, Love Dart – you can make it!'

In a last-ditch attempt to get into the final, I've entered all my fastest runners in heat number seven – the last heat of all. They are all placed in the middle of a twenty-six-inch-diameter circle, marked on a white tablecloth, and have to make their way across three intervening concentric circles to the outer perimeter. Love Dart, the tiniest of all the fifteen snails in this race, is going like the clappers, streaking across the middle circle of the thirteen-inch course. But with only two inches to go, she slows down and waves her lower tentacles about. She's been distracted by something on the dampened cloth – a green sausage looking suspiciously like a snail dropping. Meanwhile, on the other side of the circle, a great bruiser of a snail, twice the size of Love Dart, is creeping slowly but surely towards the finishing line. Suddenly he surges forward, crossing the line. Love Dart comes a respectable second, but only the winner from each heat can enter the final.

Now the heat winners are crowding round the table, preparing for the Grand Final. The owner of last year's winner, Sidney, has high hopes for this year, too. She describes the rigorous rock-and-hill-scrambling programme she devised for her newest entrant, Optimum Slime. She might possibly be exaggerating, just a little.

At a shout of 'Ready, Steady, Slow!' the finalists begin to slime across the course. The winner is the first one to poke its tentacles over the outer circle. Some stop and do a U-turn. Others cheat and hitch a ride on a fellow competitor. The race is finally won by Zoomer, the protégé of a six-year-old boy, in a very respectable three minutes and twenty-three seconds. As he is presented with his prize, the youngster's delight is almost tangible. Suddenly I am moved to tears. Sixty-odd years melt away as I remember how it all began – with the snails, and with the joy of play and discovery. Once again, I see the world through the eyes of a small child.

References

Bibliography and Source Material

Doorly, Eleanor, *The Radium Woman, A Life of Marie Curie* (William Heinemann Ltd, 1939)

Janus, H., *The Young Specialist Looks at Molluscs* (Burke, 1965)

Kerney, M. P., and Cameron, R. A. D., *A Field Guide to the Land Snails of Britain and North-West Europe* (Collins, 1979)

Williams, Peter, *Snail* (Reaktion Books, 2009)

The Conchological Society of Great Britain and Ireland, www.conchsoc.org

Further Reading

Bailey, Elisabeth Tova, *The Sound of a Wild Snail Eating* (Green Books, 2010)

Gordon, David George, *The Secret World of Slugs and Snails* (Sasquatch Books, 2010)

Acknowledgements

To all at Bloomsbury who have been involved in the production of this book, I would like to express my heartfelt thanks. I am particularly grateful to Richard Atkinson who, in helping me shape the structure and hone the text, has been both editor and mentor. I have learnt a lot. Thanks also to Rachael Oakden for her painstaking copy-editing; to Xa Shaw Stewart for all her help; to Jude Drake and Emma Daley for publicity; to proofreader Barbara Roby; and to Claire Hartigan for her care over the illustrations and cover. Special thanks are due to Natalie Hunt for coordinating all these processes so smoothly, and for her patience in answering my many queries.

I am extremely grateful to Michelle Martin, producer of the 'So You Want to be a Scientist?' project, for her constant support. I am deeply indebted to my science mentor, Dave Hodgson, for his expert guidance and his involvement in the research.

Thanks are due to Professor David Dunstan for allowing me to include his research paper; and to all the snail fans on Facebook for their encouragement and incredible homing stories. I am grateful to members of the Conchological

Society for help and support, and for delighting me with the superb photos in their journals.

To Carole, Sue, Bruce and Peter, and to St John's School, Totnes, all of whom helped out so willingly with the experiments, I am truly indebted. I also wish to acknowledge the help of Paul Morton, computer whizz, who has called round at short notice to sort out a thousand emergencies, and Totcom (Printers) of Totnes, who have come to the rescue when my printer went on strike; and to thank Linda Griffiths for her tenacity in helping me untangle my folders. Thanks too to all my friends, both gardeners and non-gardeners, who have taken such an interest in the science and who are, I hope, beginning to bond with snails; to daughter Sarah and son-in-law Chris in London for practical support, including bed-and-board; and to my grandchildren for their forbearance when I was tied to the computer and couldn't go out to play.

I am very grateful to Katy Clarke, past Chair of Swanwick Writers' Summer School who long ago recognised my need to write, and became my first mentor.

I am especially indebted to my agent, Laetitia Rutherford, who spotted a good story long before I did. Without her encouragement, this book would not have been written.

A NOTE ON THE TYPE

The text of this book is set in Fournier. Fournier is derived from the *romain du roi*, which was created towards the end of the seventeenth century for the exclusive use of the Imprimerie Royale from designs made by a committee of the Académie of Sciences. The original Fournier types were cut by the famous Paris founder Pierre Simon Fournier in about 1742. These types were some of the most influential designs of the eight and are counted among the earliest examples of the 'transitional' style of typeface. This Monotype version dates from 1924. Fournier is a light, clear face whose distinctive features are capital letters that are quite tall and bold in relation to the lower-case letters, and *decorative italics, which show the influence of the calligraphy of Fournier's time.*